Still a Pygmy

For Kangene, Nyabyamo, Muley, Kabungulu, Dorothy, and Barbara – the foundations for Pygmy activism Eastern Democratic Republic of the Congo. And for Abishay, who never got to know fully his father's story.

Ebufu bwa walundakala buna bukulu bwalu.

Still a Pygmy

A unique memoir of one man's fight to save his identity from extinction

ISAAC BACIRONGO
MICHAEL NEST

FINCH PUBLISHING
SYDNEY

Still a Pygmy: A unique memior of one man's fight to save his identity from extinction

First published in 2015 in Australia and New Zealand by Finch Publishing Pty Limited, ABN 49 057 285 248, Suite 2207, 4 Daydream Street, Warriewood, NSW, 2102, Australia.

15 8 7 6 5 4 3 2 1

There is a National Library of Australia Cataloguing-in-Publication entry available at the National Library.

Edited by Karen Gee
Editorial assistance by Megan English
Text typeset by Vicki McAuley
Cover design by Ingrid Kwong
Cover photograph by Rex Finch, iStock imagery
Printed by McPhersons Printing

Permissions: The map on pv is reproduced with permission from the University of Alabama, Alabama, USA. The map on pvi is sourced from www.cia.gov.

Map of Africa

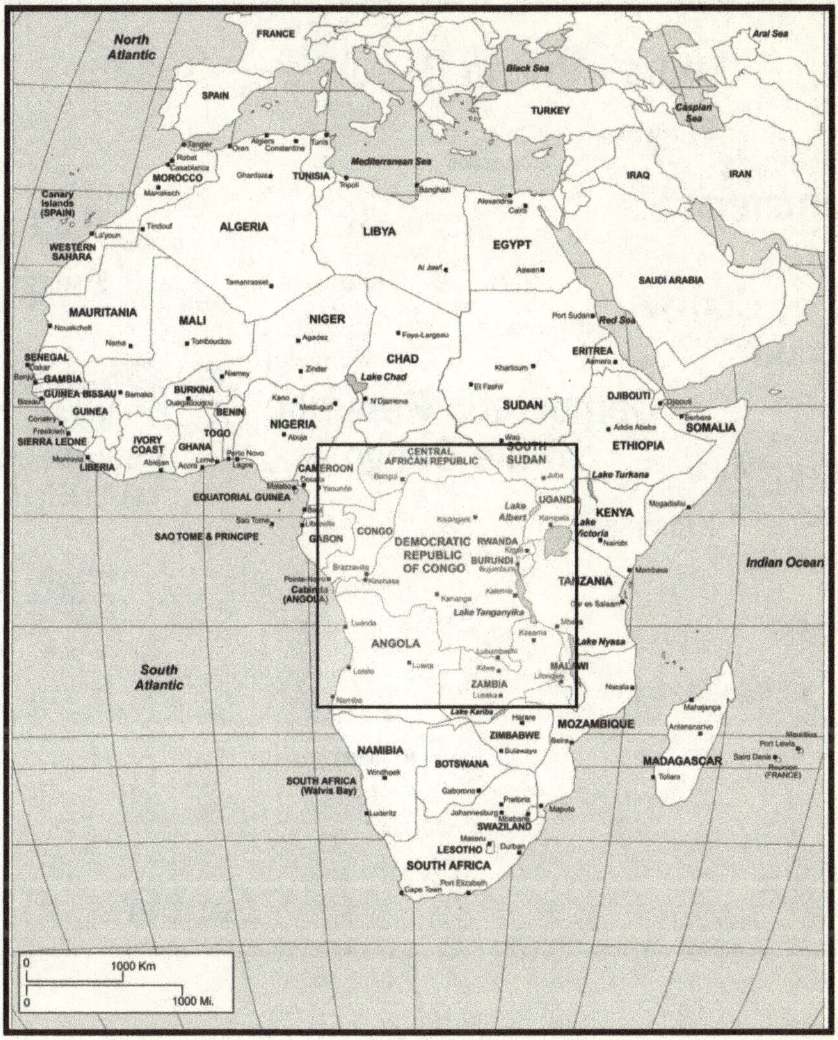

Map of the Democratic Republic of the Congo

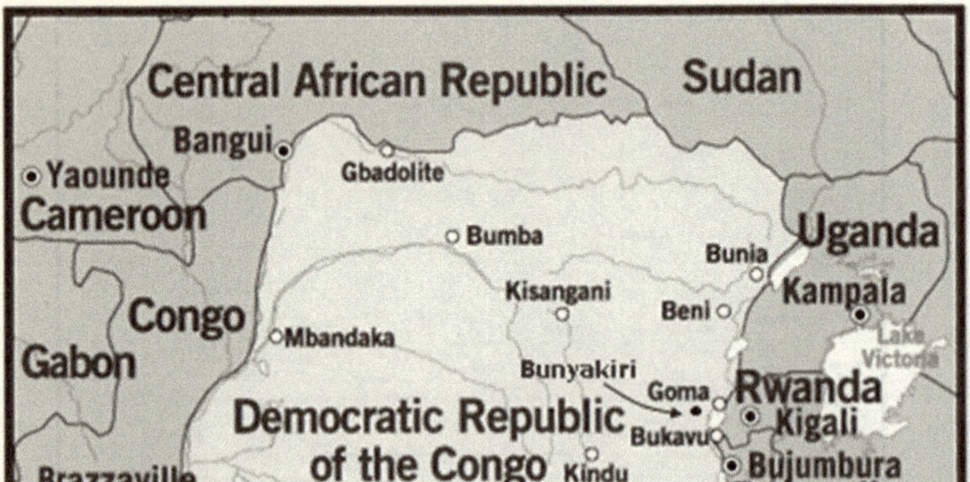

The Mafuo Chiefdom & Surrounds

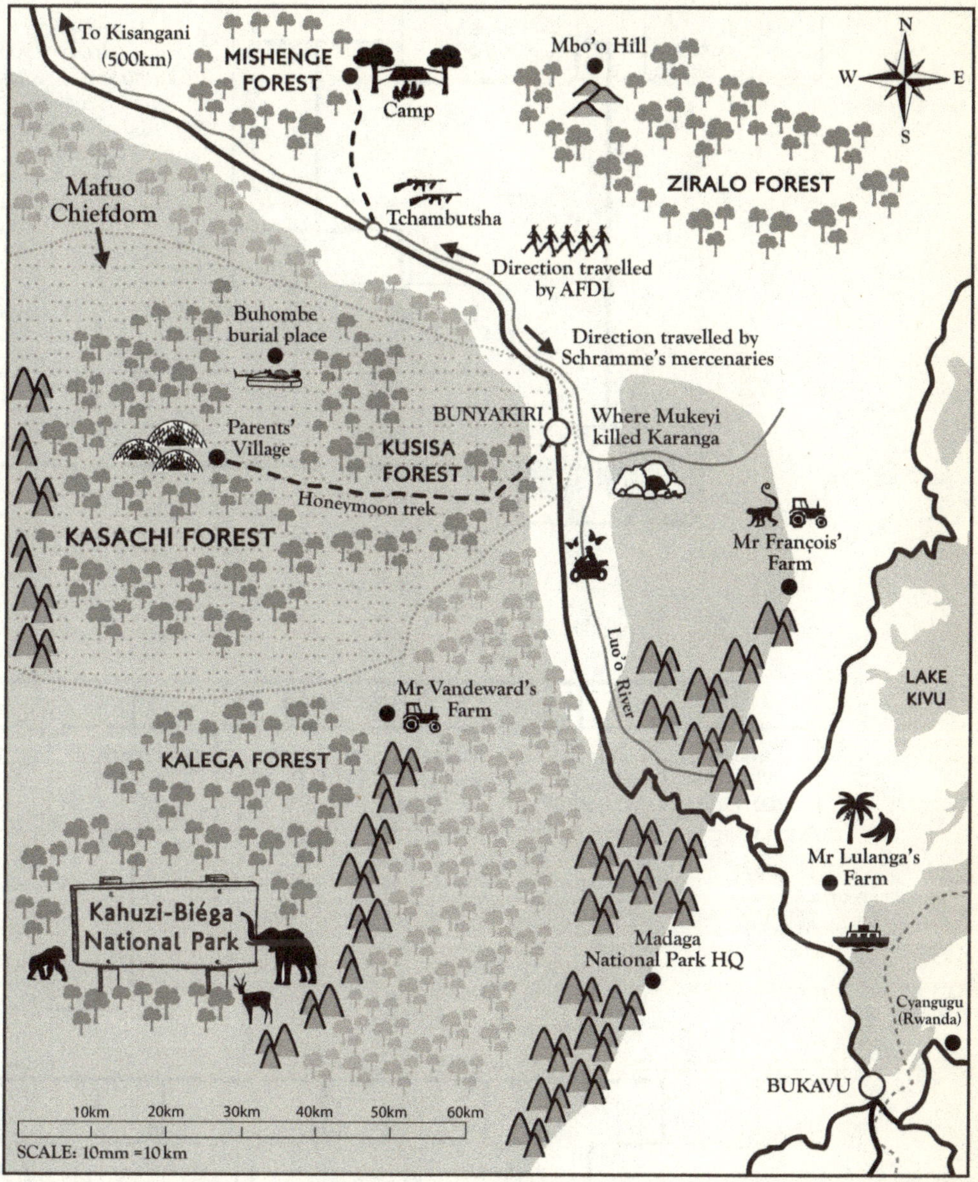

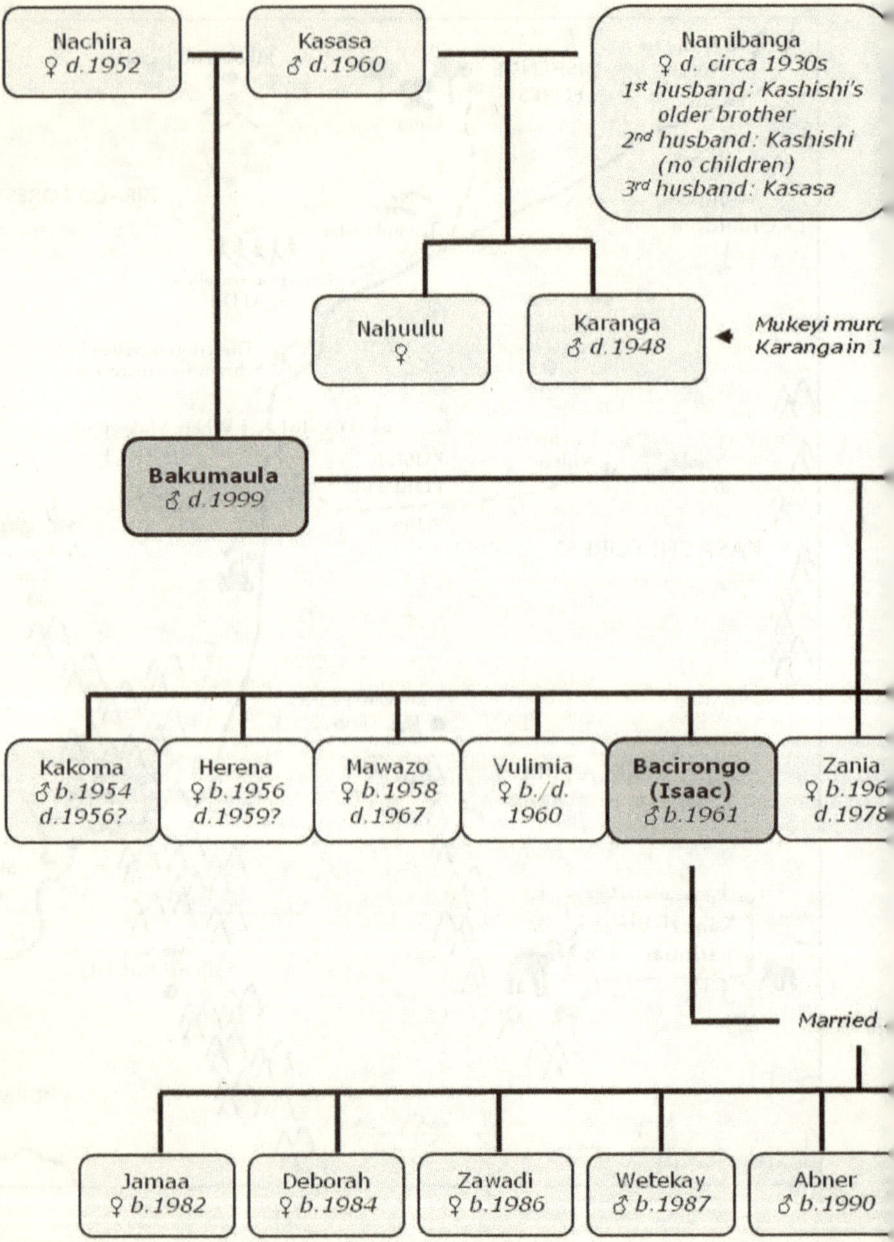
Nachira
♀ d.1952
Kasasa
♂ d.1960
Namibanga
♀ d. circa 1930s
1st husband: Kashishi's older brother
2nd husband: Kashishi (no children)
3rd husband: Kasasa
Nahuulu
♀
Karanga
♂ d.1948
Mukeyi murc
Karanga in 1
Bakumaula
♂ d.1999
Kakoma
♂ b.1954
d.1956?
Herena
♀ b.1956
d.1959?
Mawazo
♀ b.1958
d.1967
Vulimia
♀ b./d.
1960
Bacirongo
(Isaac)
♂ b.1961
Zania
♀ b.196
d.1978
Married
Jamaa
♀ b.1982
Deborah
♀ b.1984
Zawadi
♀ b.1986
Wetekay
♂ b.1987
Abner
♂ b.1990

Family Tree of Isaac Bacirongo

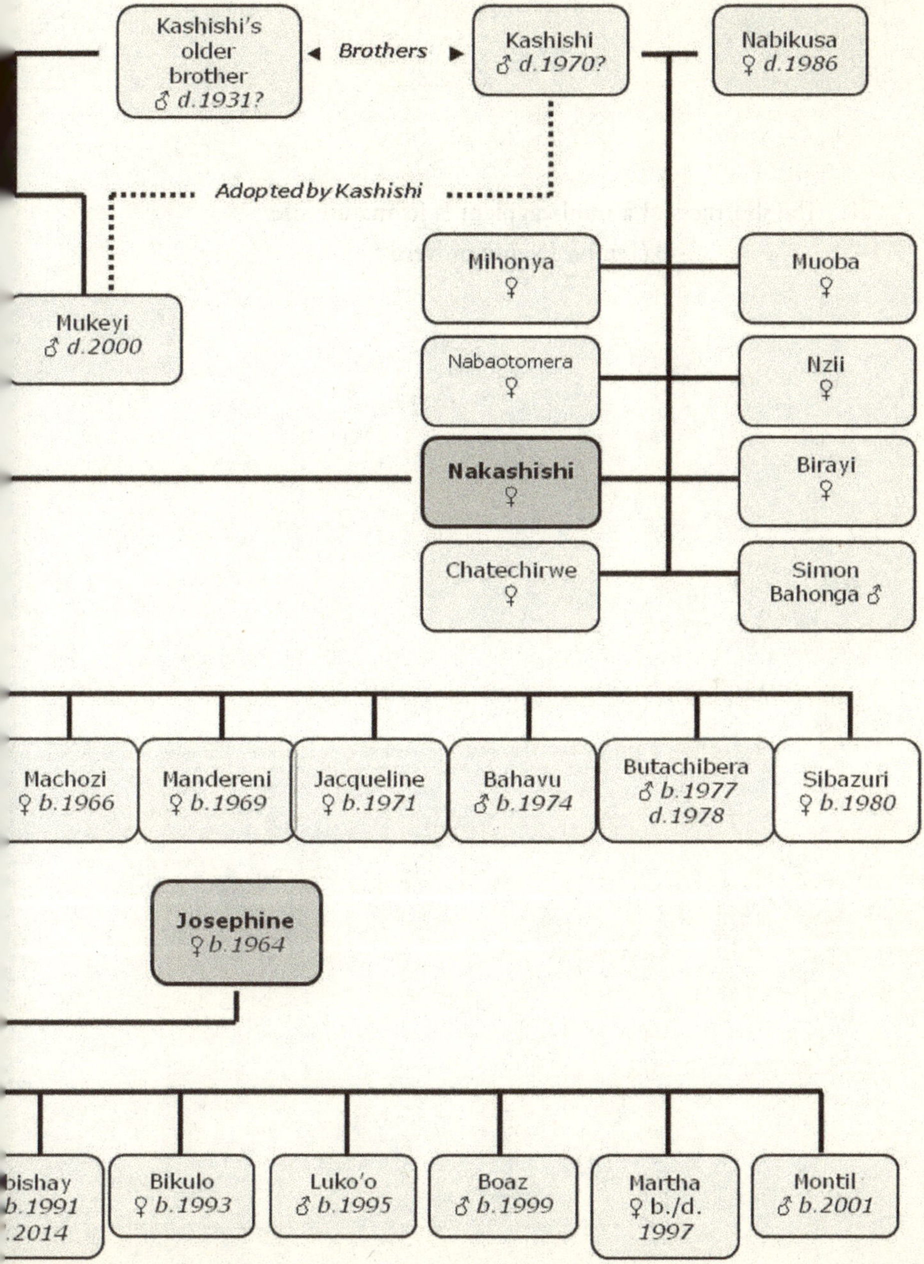

The shortness of a mini-eggplant is its mature size.
– BaTembo Pygmy proverb

Contents

Prologue: Pygmies have changed

Michael Nest

In the film adaptation of C.S. Lewis' tale *Prince Caspian: The Return to Narnia*, the Crown Prince flees on horseback when his uncle tries to murder him and take over the throne. Prince Caspian is pursued by soldiers but they hesitate to follow him into the dark woods, held back by fear and superstitions of the 'Old Narnians' who once lived there: minotaurs, fauns, dancing trees, talking animals and dwarves. Prince Caspian, knocked unconscious in the forest when he falls off his horse, is given shelter by a dwarf and a badger. When he regains consciousness and sees his hosts he starts in fright: 'What are you?' he exclaims. 'I mean, you're Narnians. You're supposed to be extinct!'

When I told people I was working on a memoir of a Pygmy, they reacted as if I had just told them that Old Narnians still exist. There was amazement that a Pygmy lives in Sydney; wonder that Pygmies really do exist at all; intense curiosity about stature (so let's clarify this right now: Isaac is short); and sometimes mirth at how exotic the whole thing sounded. I'm embarrassed to say that initially I fed some of this. 'Guess what I did on the weekend?' I asked one friend. 'Had lunch with a Pygmy.' 'Should you be calling him that?' she shot back. Another friend told me she thought the word 'Pygmy' simply reflected an imperial prejudice towards short Africans, not realising there were whole populations – Isaac would say a whole race – who identify as such. Saying I was working on a memoir of a Pygmy was the most straightforward way to explain the project, but that simple word 'Pygmy' provoked the Narnian response.

Legends and fairytales about short people who live in wild places – dwarves, hobbits, Pygmies – are deep within our subconscious and they make us doubt what is real. This is even more the case for Pygmies because they live in the rainforest of tropical Africa. I have flown over Central Africa and, from above, the forest is impenetrable: a thick green canopy that goes on for thousands of miles, blanketing everything in mystery. We know something of the jungle: it is where malaria and Ebola come from, where strange animals live and where Marlow from Joseph Conrad's *Heart of Darkness* journeyed. We wonder what Pygmies could be doing there, out of sight.

Some stories about Pygmies are so outlandish we can hardly believe they are real. Indigenous people everywhere have been mistreated, but surely the single most demeaning thing ever done to an indigenous person was to a Pygmy called Ota Benga. In 1906, he was put with an orang-utan into the Monkey House at the Bronx Zoo in New York and made into an exhibit. The zoo director's intention was to provoke New Yorkers into reflecting on Darwin's theory of evolution and arguments about the Missing Link … and to make the turnstiles spin. A century later the international media reported that armed militias waging war in the Democratic Republic of the Congo ('the Congo' or simply 'Congo' as Isaac commonly refers to it) were hunting down Pygmies to eat them, in order to obtain the magical powers that reportedly allow Pygmies to survive in the forests. A former colleague of Isaac's, also a Pygmy, went to the United Nations in New York to plead for cannibalism to be explicitly included as a crime against humanity, so perpetrators could be fully prosecuted. Cannibalism was not at that stage designated as such, but who would have thought it needed to be?

The truth about Pygmy life in the forest, as Isaac recounts in this memoir, is somewhat more prosaic than all the myths, stories and legends. In the forest Isaac led a contented childhood that was relentlessly focused on gathering food. But few Pygmies live exclusively in the forest. Most move in and out of the jungle depending on the season, bartering meat, honey or their labour in return for food. Most are also no longer the hunter-gatherers untouched by modernity that we might wish.

The idea that Pygmies are a pre-modern people in a 'lost world' has excited travellers and scholars ever since colonisation by Europeans in the late nineteenth century made the forests of equatorial Africa accessible. Colonisation happened at the same time that Darwin's theory of evolution was sweeping popular culture, and much of the original scholarly interest in Pygmies was focused on obtaining evidence about their place in the presumed hierarchy of human races. Academia has subsequently evolved, but Pygmies' short stature and their hunter-gatherer ways remain perennially favourite subjects, and anthropologists, human biologists, geneticists and linguists have written libraries about these topics.

In all our meetings the subject that irritated Isaac the most was the idea that Pygmies live in a forest idyll or that they are incapable of adapting to life outside the jungle. 'All these academics,' he would rail, 'they write as though Pygmies can only live in the forest.' Isaac often listed the Pygmies he knew with jobs and education. Indeed, an increasing number of Pygmies live in the towns and cities of Central Africa. Others in the east of the

Democratic Republic of the Congo, driven out of the countryside by war, live almost destitute on the edges of those towns and cities. And some Pygmies move to Australia.

I first met Isaac in 2009, six years after he came to Sydney. I was doing research for a book on the politics around an obscure mineral called tantalite, or 'coltan' as it is known in Congo. A Congolese geologist told me about a friend of his, a former coltan trader from Eastern Congo now living in Sydney. 'He's a Pygmy too,' the geologist added. I had met Pygmies before when I was backpacking through Africa and I had done research in Congo, so I knew something about them. But like those friends and acquaintances who gave the 'Old Narnian' response, I wondered how on earth a Pygmy had washed up on the shores of Sydney.

I telephoned Isaac and told him about my coltan book project, and he invited me around for lunch. We sat in his large living room which, African style, had several lounge settees placed around the walls to accommodate many guests, but few other decorations. His wife, Josephine, fried pork chops and greens in the kitchen, well within earshot but keeping silent. Isaac's courteous children – he has ten – came up to me in turn, greeting me and telling me their name and number: 'Hello, I'm Abishay. Number six.' 'Boaz. I'm number nine.' I was transported back to the family homes and hospitality of Congo.

I found in Isaac someone with whom I could talk about Congolese politics, and felt grateful. I realise now that Isaac was also grateful to have found someone with whom he could talk about books and ideas. Isaac had had some problems in the workplace and he welcomed the opportunity to discuss these with an Australian who understood local work culture as well. I was interested in his perspective, as a Pygmy, on life, but the more we talked the more I realised how idiosyncratic Isaac is. I knew no other Pygmies with whom I could compare him, but I knew the stereotypes and I had met many Congolese. By Isaac's own account he is different. He is his own man, someone who questions things and insists on coming to his own conclusions, sometimes coming a cropper in the process when he has queried powerful people. As I came to discover, he is also unlike other Pygmies in that he has resisted hiding his racial and ethnic identity, although he has at times. As we relaxed in each other's company Isaac told me more and more about his life and I became convinced it was a story worth telling to a larger audience.

In early 2012, Isaac emailed me some pages of a memoir he had started drafting, wanting feedback. He had also started to tell me more about his life in Congo. Isaac had a compelling personal story, with tales of ruthless social competition, his mother engaging witchdoctors to kill her daughter-in-law (Isaac's wife), and of working as a human rights activist under a repressive regime. However, in its current form I thought his manuscript was unlikely to find a publisher. I offered to co-write a full memoir with Isaac with a view to publication, and he agreed.

Our project faced several obstacles. Isaac's family, not wanting to be 'outed' as Pygmies, has not supported it. Like Pygmies back in Africa who try to disguise their identity and assimilate in order to avoid discrimination, his family has tried to do the same in Australia. It is hard enough being black Africans in an Australia still getting used to African migrants, let alone being Pygmies. His wife cautioned, 'We should try to live a simple life. When you write a book you don't see anything wrong with it, but in one or two years the consequences may start to come.' She gently reminded Isaac that it was his decision to become an activist and give public talks that had caused the family to flee to Kenya and become refugees, bringing an end to their comfortable life in Congo. His children told him, 'If you come to Australia you should be Australian. We should forget about all these things from Africa.'

Isaac has also been fearful that publishing his story would bring humiliation and contempt upon his family; that people – readers of this memoir, other Africans, Australians – would dismiss his stories of struggle. I was taken aback that he genuinely thought he might be disparaged for telling his story. I suggested we give a presentation about the project at an African studies conference, feeling sure that everyone there would be supportive and interested. The conference's theme was to 'explore ways in which Africans on the continent and abroad continue to change, challenge and reshape our knowledge of African people, spaces and places'. Isaac loved it. 'This is really fantastic,' he emailed. 'When I looked at the program, I was so happy to see that the theme of the conference matches exactly with our fight against false ideology – that Pygmies are still the same and have never changed towards modern civilisation. I hope my memoir will make Pygmies be proud of their identity and make other people understand Pygmies are also world citizens with the same capabilities as anyone.' A friend took a photo of us presenting at the conference and it captures Isaac in full flight. Dressed in a crisp blue-and-white striped shirt he is speaking passionately, kind brown eyes and high forehead crinkled in animation above gesticulating hands, a tuft of grey in his black hair revealing that his perspective is one of a mature man, a father, who has seen a lot of life.

His family had cautioned him about going to the conference. 'Just remember,' Josephine said, 'that saying publicly at a conference that we are oppressed is why we are in Australia today. You should be careful talking about rights to this and that person. That is very dangerous.' She was referring to Isaac attending conferences in Africa when he had been an activist and talking about the dire situation of Pygmies. 'We already had to run from Congo. If the Australian government doesn't like what you say, where can we run to next? There is nowhere left.' Again I was taken aback, this time by the idea that there might be retribution by the Australian government, even though the whole family are now Australian citizens. These comments told me something about the deep fear within Congolese who have learnt never to trust government authorities, who have betrayed and abused them for 130 years. Even after obtaining Australian citizenship, Isaac and his wife do not fully believe they have rights that allow them to speak their mind and which might protect them.

Isaac can also fall into melancholy and this occasionally, if temporarily, tempered his enthusiasm for the project. Even when he emailed those first draft pages to me, he wrote: 'I started writing my memoir. You can have a look at the introduction attached to this email. I am expressively very exhausted and I have no strength, otherwise I could have written half of this book already despite my poor English. I have become sleepless, thinking and asking myself a lot of questions in regard to what I experienced in the past and now.'

Ultimately Isaac's desire to write a memoir and tackle the past outweighed his doubts. 'I told Josephine I want our kids and our grandkids to know me. To know why we migrated from Africa to Australia. If it is not written down, everything will be forgotten.'

Another motivation was to counter the stereotypes and myths about Pygmies. 'Pygmies have changed,' Isaac told me. 'They are not the same as they used to be. If you go to Google Images and search for "Pygmies" you will get pictures of Pygmies in the forest only, not Pygmies who are educated, who are modern. Just those who are half-naked and live a traditional life.'

Recording Isaac's story was straightforward. We met once or twice a week over coffee at a café in a suburb halfway between our homes, or occasionally at the local pub. The Korean café owners indulged us, kindly letting us sit there for hours. Each time we met I was transported to other times and places by Isaac's stories; so engrossed, I barely noticed the ebb and flow of other customers around our table. Once Isaac opened up on a theme, I just had to keep pace taking handwritten notes – copying his words down verbatim – and asking for the occasional clarification. Isaac is a good storyteller, and a patient one, and he became accustomed to talking at the speed at which I could write. When I got home, I would sit down at the computer and type up my notes from that day.

In getting Isaac to talk about his life I made him recall some terrible events, and I still feel badly about this. But there were also some beautiful moments when my questions led Isaac to recall the many people who'd helped or inspired him. One of them was an Aboriginal woman, Letty Scott, who passed away in 2009. Because Letty was Aboriginal, and because we wanted to include some words she had told Isaac about her personal experiences with white people, I thought we should get permission from a family member to use her name and repeat these words. I did an Internet search to try to track down contact details for her family, and found a

Facebook page with a photo of a Letty Scott who died in 2009. I felt this must be Isaac's friend, and emailed him the link. Isaac sent me the following message in reply: 'This is unbelievable, I had no idea that Letty's picture could be found on Facebook. Letty's picture makes us all cry in my family, tears are still falling from my eyes. I heard her voice last when she rang me in 2007. I remember how she used to hold my hand, touching me and telling me emotional, encouraging words.'

Jan Vansina, an eminent scholar of Central African societies, lamented that:

> There are no Pygmy authors and no authors who come from the villages with which the hunter-gatherers are linked. The main reason that Pygmies have attracted such attention has been, first, their 'exotic' appeal, and second, the assumption that somehow they represent the roots of humanity. They are studied for their presumed potential to elucidate life at the dawn of humanity, not for their own sake.

So here is a book by a Pygmy author, a memoir about himself and his people, in his own words, for his own sake. Although as Isaac says, 'Of course, this is my personal story. It is not the story of all Pygmies or even all the Pygmies from Eastern Congo.' The book is a collaboration in that Isaac told me his story and I recorded it, but the text is 99 per cent in Isaac's original words – unchanged from the stories he told me in the café. My role was to shift sentences around, order topics to shape the narrative and elicit background information about events to provide context for what was happening to Isaac. We have changed several names to protect identities.

Compared to fellow Australians, Isaac's life has been strange, for sure. But what has most shaped his life is not exotic at all. It is those utterly contemporary and universal themes of love, ambition, pride and prejudice.

1

Because of what happened in 1948

In 1948 my mum's brother murdered my dad's brother. Mama was given to Papa to be his wife, as compensation to Dad's family for the murder. That is how my parents got together.

Why this happened is a long story. It is the story of my family's beginning.

My mother's father was called Kashishi. He was well known and unlike other Pygmies, he did not run away from white people when they came to our forest. He worked for them. Grandpa Kashishi had an older brother, but he died before my mother was born and no-one can remember his name.

Grandpa Kashishi's older brother had a wife, Namibanga. They had one son together, Mukeyi. Mukeyi was two years old when his father died. In Pygmy culture, when a man dies, his wife is taken in and looked after by his brother, as his wife. In this way, Grandpa Kashishi came to be married to Namibanga and he adopted his nephew, Mukeyi, as his son.

Grandpa Kashishi and Namibanga did not get on. Kashishi got tired of her and kicked her out. During Kashishi's time the custom to separate was for the husband to make a cord called a *muungu* and present it to his wife. *Muungu* are made from forest lianas and are rolled back and forth on the thigh until they are twisted into a cord. When a husband gives a *muungu* to his wife, this tells her that she will be seen as just a sister; there will be no more sexual relations. Kashishi gave Namibanga a *muungu* and she left.

Grandpa Kashishi got another wife after Namibanga left – Nabikusa, my mother's mum. Grandma Nabikusa was a short, solid woman. I got my shape from her. She was skilful in catching crabs and fish in the rivers, and an expert in digging wild yams – we call them birrongo – and gathering wild fruits and honey. Grandpa Kashishi and Grandma Nabikusa had seven daughters and one son. My mother, one of the seven daughters, is called Nakashishi, which means 'daughter of Kashishi'. Mukeyi became a step-brother to their family because he stayed with Grandpa Kashishi even though his mother had left. Although he was really her cousin, Mama calls Mukeyi her brother because they were raised as brother and sister.

On the other side of my family is my father's father, Grandpa Kasasa. He had only one child – Bakomaula, my father – with his first wife. Grandpa Kasasa wanted more children so sought a second wife. Having more than one wife was common back then and every man wanted lots of children. After Grandpa Kashishi kicked out Namibanga, Grandpa Kasasa took her in to be his second wife.

Grandpa Kasasa was a tough man. He was known as an avenger: if you did something wrong to him, he would pay you back. In the 1930s his family had a dispute with the family of Katfumbi, a local man, over hunting access to a forest. Someone from Katfumbi's family killed someone from Grandpa's family, so Grandpa Kasasa went to Katfumbi's camp and speared Katfumbi's wife, Namadaga. She was pregnant with twins, and she and the babies died.

After Grandpa Kasasa took in Namibanga she had two children with him. The first was a girl, Nahuulu; the second was a boy, Karanga. Namibanga died when her children, including Mukeyi, were young. None of them can remember her.

After Grandpa Kasasa died, my aunt Nahuulu got married. She was about fifteen. In Pygmy culture, a man who wants a wife has to pay a dowry to the girl's family – a bride-price. These days the man usually gives cash, but in the old days – before the Belgians came and colonised Congo – there was a kind of money used in the forest called *butea*. Africans traditionally used *butea* as money before coins and notes came along. *Butea* was made from copper wire that was twisted into a bracelet, and inside it was the thread of the raffia plant. *Butea* was difficult to make and difficult to find. Metal smiths were very rare in the forest and there was a lot of craftwork involved to make *butea*. You could tell if someone was rich because they wore a lot of *butea* bracelets. Many Pygmies in my area of Congo used *butea* for dowries. If they did not use *butea*, or did not have any, a man would just say, 'If you want to marry my daughter bring me a hunting dog or bring us some meat.'

Families keep a dowry until one of their sons needs it for his own marriage, when it is used by him for his dowry. Grandpa Kasasa died before Aunt Nahuulu got married, which meant there was no man to look after Nahuulu's dowry on behalf of his family. This was the start of the problem. Karanga, as Nahuulu's full brother, had the right of custody over the dowry but he was still too young – perhaps not even a teenager. There was a dispute in the family over who should control it. Whoever had custody of the dowry would be able to use it to pay for his own bride.

Mukeyi, who had the same mother as Karanga but a different father, told Karanga: 'I will keep that dowry for you until you find a wife.' My dad also told Karanga, 'We have the same father, so I'll keep the dowry until you get married.' But Karanga decided to give the dowry to Mukeyi to look after, because they had been in the same womb and grew up together, and he had more affection for Mukeyi than Papa.

That same year, Mukeyi started to plan how to kill Karanga so he could keep the dowry. Everyone told Karanga that Mukeyi would never give back the dowry money, so Karanga started to ask Mukeyi about the dowry and where he had hidden it. Mukeyi got annoyed by Karanga's questions and told Karanga that he had hidden the money in a small cave under a boulder near a waterfall in the forest. Mukeyi took Karanga to see the place, and told him to look inside. When Karanga put his head in the cave, Mukeyi stabbed him four times with a lance.

Back in the village, when it became dark, people started asking, 'Where is Mukeyi? Where is Karanga?' The next day they started looking but couldn't find either of them. Someone remembered that they had gone to the waterfall, so they went there and found Karanga's body. Mukeyi had run away.

In the evening, news spread throughout the village that Karanga had been murdered. People could not believe that he was dead. Karanga was a healthy, growing, young man and had been seen by many people throughout the day. It was a death that made people choke.

In the old days, when there were no radios or telephones, people who were good singers would make up songs about an event and these were sung from village to village as a way of passing on news. Someone in the village made up a song in Swahili to mourn Karanga's death, and this song spread far. It was still sung when I was a child, many years later.

Kufa kwa mtu si mbali
Kufa kwa mtu si mbali
Karanga alikata roho mama yooo

Somebody's death can be so easy like this?
Somebody's death can be so easy like this?
Karanga has breathed his last.

My wife, Josephine, told me when I married her that her sister-in-law used to sing these words. Josephine never imagined that one day she would marry someone from the family in that song.

The Kasasa family became very angry when Karanga was murdered. Some family members went to Mukeyi's father, Grandpa Kashishi, and told him, 'Your son killed our son, so you have to pay, otherwise we will kill someone from your family.' When someone from the Kasasa family made a threat, people knew they meant it. Grandpa Kashishi's family gave my mum, Nakashishi, to my dad's family as payment. That's how Papa came to marry Mama.

Mukeyi was on the run for three years. He was arrested in 1951 by the colonial police, put on trial, convicted of murder and sent to prison in the city of Kisangani in central Congo. In 1960 when Congo became independent from Belgium, there was an amnesty for prisoners, including murderers, and Mukeyi was released. He died about fourteen years ago. Because Grandpa Kashishi's family had already settled the debt with my father's family there were no major problems between us, but occasionally there was some anger. Mukeyi's son called me once and suggested that Karanga's murder was still a problem. I told him that he wasn't even born when Karanga was killed and neither was I. In my mind it no longer mattered.

But it was always a problem for Mama. She was probably around thirteen or fourteen at the time, although we do not know when Mama was born, and she was not happy about being given as compensation to someone she barely knew. Grandpa Kashishi and Grandma Nabikusa forced her to marry Papa just so one of their family members wouldn't be killed in revenge for Karanga's death. They only had one son, and they thought the Kasasa family might kill him if they did not give their daughter. But Mama thought she was not owed to Papa and did not see why he should be paid any compensation because Papa was not a full brother of Karanga. Also, Mama did not like Papa – he was not her choice of a man.

2

People of the forest

I was born on a Sunday in 1961 on the farm of Monsieur Vandeward. Like other Pygmy families, depending on the season, Mama and Papa left the forest to find work in villages and on farms. One of the farms on which Papa found work was that of Monsieur Vandeward. He was a Belgian who had come into the area and cleared the forest to make a cinchona plantation. Quinine, which is used to fight malaria, is extracted from cinchona plants. When Congo became independent in 1960, some Belgians chose to stay rather than leave, and Monsieur Vandeward was one of those who stayed. Papa cleared vegetation and pruned the cinchona plants on his plantation.

Just after I was born, some women living on the farm heard that Mama had had a baby and came to visit her. Because it was a Sunday they told Mama she should name me Lwamungu, which literally means 'day of God' – Sunday – in KiTembo. And she did. So I am called Lwamungu. Mama also gave me another name: Bacirongo. The letter 'c' in KiTembo is pronounced 'ch' as in 'church', so my name is pronounced 'Ba*ch*irongo'. Cirongo means 'family line' and Bacirongo means 'from the family'.

My parents had twelve children. Before me there was an older brother and three older sisters, but they all died young and I became the eldest. My second eldest sister, Mawazo, died when I was five or six. Mama gave her medicine against worms, but she made the mixture too strong and Mawazo died. After me, my parents had seven more children: two boys and five girls.

We know our birth dates because when Papa started working for Monsieur Vandeward, he was given a little yellow booklet. Officially it was called a *livre de travail*, or work book, but in Swahili, we called it *ketabu muzungu* or 'white man's book'. Papa had no idea what was written in it because he could not read. He just knew he had to have it. Monsieur Vandeward's manager recorded information about Papa in the book, including our birth dates. In the mid-1970s the government introduced identity cards for citizens, so Papa threw away that old white man's book.

Mama and Papa's marriage was not really faithful. Mum did not like Dad and started having boyfriends. She left him many times and went to live with different men. Whenever she left Papa, her family took her back to him, worried that Grandpa Kasasa's family would kill someone from their family as payback for Karanga's death if she didn't stay. One story in the family is that another reason Mama had boyfriends was because Dad was weak and Mum needed boyfriends to satisfy her desires. Once a man in our village started to have affection for me, and when I cut my foot he gave me some money to go to the clinic. I thought he was just being kind, but I discovered later he was Mama's boyfriend. My grandmother pointed him out to me and said, 'That man took your mother from your dad.'

Because Mama was having boyfriends during her married life, we are not sure, biologically, who our fathers are. Dad had mistresses as well, and so we are not exactly sure how many children he had either. We were never really close to Papa because Mama didn't like him much and did not spend a lot of time with him. We might live with him for six months, but then Mama would get fed up and go elsewhere in the forest and we would go with her. However, in the year before I was born, my parents and grandparents led a nomadic life together, in a green and mountainous area of dense forest with bamboo and giant, fragrant trees. This is the Kalega Forest. They moved from place to place to hunt and gather food just as Pygmies had for generations.

We are BaTembo Pygmies and, like other Pygmies, we are people of the forest. According to our mythology, when other people who are not Pygmies – we call them Bantu – came to Central Africa, they came from the north and found Pygmies already there. My own ancestors roamed in the forests from Kahuzi up to Walikale and into the forests of Shabunda. This is where you can find the Kalega Forest. The region is very mountainous and the smaller villages are in deep forest and reachable only on dirt paths.

Bantu from many tribes came into our land centuries ago, but before the seventeenth century nobody could talk about BaTembo people for the simple reason that they did not exist. About 400 years ago one of those Bantu men called Katembo came into our land. He was the son of Kifamandu, and probably from the Hunde tribe. Katembo fell in love with a Pygmy woman. (I have never heard her name – BaTembo people only want to remember Katembo, not the name of their Pygmy ancestor, so everyone has forgotten her.) Katembo's family was very upset with him because they believed that intermarriage with Pygmies could bring a curse on the entire family, and Katembo was banished. Katembo and his wife made a new settlement at Mbo'o Hill, in an area now called Ufamandu, and had many sons and daughters.

From Mbo'o Hill the Katembo family spread out and became a big clan. In every new settlement they met Pygmies with whom they intermarried and who they came to consider as cousins. They all lived and worked together peacefully, going together into the forest to collect food. One thing we BaTembo all have in common now is that, like full-blood Pygmies, BaTembo can disguise themselves so well in the forest that they can be passed without ever being noticed. From this mixing of Pygmies and Bantu from the Hunde tribe, a new tribe was born: the BaTembo – named after the Katembo family.

Thousands of years ago Pygmies had their own language, but today Pygmies speak the language of the Bantu tribes around them and the BaTembo speak KiTembo. Some people say KiTembo is really just Hunde spoken badly. In KiTembo the word for Pygmy is Batfwa, which means something like 'outsider'. The word Pygmy itself is not an African word. It comes from Ancient Greek myths where it was used to describe a tribe of dwarfs that lived in Africa and India.

The word 'Bantu' means 'human' in the languages spoken in Congo. Pygmies are never described as Bantu. We are never 'humans'. Some Bantu think we are more related to chimpanzees. Mama told me, 'Since I was born no-one has considered Pygmies as people. Don't think that one day in this world you will be treated as a full human being, or with dignity. You'll only be treated with dignity in a place where they don't know you.'

My family's traditional country is in the Mafuo Pygmy Chiefdom and is called Bunyakiri, but this is a new name. Around 1900 the first white man arrived in the area. He asked a village chief, someone we call a *mwami*, to find him men who could cut down the forest because he wanted to build an office. The *mwami* brought him some short young men who had axes. When the white man saw them he was amazed at their small size and did not believe they were capable of cutting down giant trees. The white man asked the *mwami* the name of the hill on which he wanted to build his office. As there were no interpreters, the *mwami* misunderstood and thought the white man was asking him if those little men were able to cut the trees. The *mwami*, answering in our KiTembo language, said *Ee bunyakiri Musungu, utabulolaaku bacha*, which in English means, 'Yes white man, they are strong, don't mind their small size.' The white man then named the hill 'Bunyakiri', which actually means 'small strong men'.

That *mwami* was not a Pygmy because traditionally Pygmies have no chiefs; chiefdoms are for those BaTembo who are Bantu, not the BaTembo who are Pygmies. We have an expression – *Batfwa bateira mwami*, or Pygmies have no chiefs – because this kind of chiefdom arrangement does not exist in Pygmy culture. If there are disputes or decisions need to be made, a small number of male elders do this. For example, if we have killed an antelope and want to divide it up, an elder will decide who will get what piece of meat, depending on whether they were the one who stabbed the antelope with a spear, or owned the hunting dog, or carried the nets.

We only started to have chiefs in the 1940s. At that time, one of the chiefs of the Shi tribe sent someone to govern the area where we lived, to be our chief. The BaTembo said we didn't want a Shi chief, but the Belgian colonial administrator wanted help ruling us and supported the Shi chief. The BaTembo eventually started to select their own chiefs after that.

So the BaTembo are a hybrid tribe made up of Bantus, Pygmies and people who are mixed Pygmy–Bantu – and now we have chiefs. Where I am from, BaTembo and Pygmies are one people, undividable, although some Bantu people might not like me saying that.

The Belgians tried to get Pygmies out of the forest and make us live in Bantu villages, so we would become workers. We did not like that! Because of pressure from the Belgians, in the 1940s and 1950s some families moved out of the forest but left their eldest sons behind in the deep forest where the Belgians could not find them. After Congo became independent in 1960 we all went back.

Because of discrimination Pygmies do whatever they can to hide their identity and pass as a Bantu. My parents told me that whenever someone asks our tribe, I should say we are BaTembo. My parents never said they were Pygmies. This did not always work. Sometimes it can be hard to differentiate a Pygmy from a Bantu by appearance because of mixing, but there are clues. Bantu have an adage: *Utachiakanaa e'butfwa n'ebunu bubumbure*. 'Don't deny you are a Pygmy, because your lips betray you.' They say this because, unlike Bantu, who have thick lips, Pygmies have thin lips. Pygmies also blink fast, especially the women. A friend of mine, a Pygmy, was visiting Bukavu, the provincial capital of South Kivu, one day, saw a woman blinking very fast. He asked her if she was a Pygmy. She said, 'Oh! You could tell?!' When Pygmies marry Bantu, over time their physical characteristics change. They get taller, their lips get bigger and they blink more slowly.

Even though Pygmies are marginalised, we have a special role in Bantu culture because of our connection to the spirit world. Traditionally Pygmies believed in a creator god who created the forest and everything in it, and that the forest was full of the spirits of ancestors who had died. We also believed that anyone who helped us or protected us was like a god. For example, if a tree protected us from lightning, we believed that tree was like a god. Bantu and missionaries said we were pagans and we started to change our thinking, but Pygmies still have ceremonies when we do various things to make spirits happy, and we perform these ceremonies for Bantu as well. For example, before going hunting, Pygmies might perform a ceremony to help catch something. If they do not catch anything, despite having done a ceremony, they might attribute this to some flaw in the ceremony rather than think that perhaps the ceremony was useless.

The most important ceremonial roles Pygmies held in Bantu culture were when a *mwami* was put on the throne and when he died. The Bantu were afraid that if they did not give Pygmies a role in these ceremonies it would anger the ancestral spirits of the land. Bantus believe that ancestral spirits respond better to Pygmies because Pygmies are the people of the forest, so Bantu call on us to participate in rituals, in activities concerning the forest and to stop natural disasters. When something like a destructive storm happens, BaTembo would say it was because the spirits were upset that Pygmies were not given a proper role in a ceremony that happened earlier, sometimes years earlier.

Many years ago, before I was born, there was a calamitous storm in the Kalima Chiefdom, which neighbours my area. People said the storm happened because the *mwami* did not have a Pygmy wife, so a young Pygmy girl, Nanzibiro, was given to him. The problem was that they did not get on; the *mwami* only married Nanzibiro because he was afraid of the spirits and feared another calamity. The *mwami* preferred his other wife, who was a Bantu, but Nanzabiro was happy because she thought she was now the queen.

3

When leopards were our only enemy

In 1967 a white mercenary from Belgium, Jean Schramme, and his 'Leopard Battalion' advanced along the road near where we were living. He hoped to capture Bukavu and eventually take over the whole country. I still remember how my family fled to escape Schramme. We heard shooting and were scared of being caught up in the conflict, so fled from Mr Vandeward's farm into the deep forest.

Pygmies know how to live in the forest, so we could always find food and build huts, and we were protected. Normally Pygmies move in and out of the forest, but this time we stayed for a whole year because we were scared of leaving.

Life was very social in the forest. The small camps we lived in had about five or six different huts, with about twenty people in each camp, and everyone in the camp was related. A big family will have a big camp, and a small family will have a small camp. Perhaps 500 metres away from our camp would be the camp of another family.

Mama and Papa never owned a permanent house and had no idea how to build one. We lived in small domed huts made of a stick frame covered in leaves. The huts didn't have any doors because no-one had any possessions to protect, just a couple of cooking pots. When they decided to move to a new area, they abandoned the old hut and built a new one. It took Mum and Dad about four hours to make a hut. If you were careful and made a strong frame you could make a hut that lasted a year. If there was heavy rain the water came right down through the trees to the ground, but if there was only a little rain we would get only a few drops on the ground. We dug a small channel around the outside of our hut to drain water away when it rained.

The entrance to our home was very low, perhaps a metre high. Even short people like me had to bend to get in. Bigger huts might have a wall that created a sleeping space for parents. We sometimes cooked inside by making a fire in the middle of three stones and resting a pot on top. There were no chairs or tables. Everyone sat on a log or on the ground. My parents liked living in this kind of hut. Many years later I bought them twenty sheets of iron to cover their roof instead of leaves, but they exchanged it for meat. They were happy with their traditional hut and having assets like iron sheeting was meaningless to them.

Mama and Papa encouraged us to do some chores, like bringing water from the river in a gourd or calabash. Mama used to give extra meat to the child who brought water, and this is how we were rewarded for doing something good or useful – with meat. If I was naughty, such as when I fought with my sisters, I'd be beaten by Mum or Dad. I remember that once I was running to the river to get water, when I fell and dropped the gourd I was carrying and it broke. It would have taken seven or eight months to grow another gourd, and it costs money to buy a new one at the market, so breaking it was a bad thing to do. Mama beat me for that, because she said I was just playing and did not believe that I had tripped and fallen.

Everything in the forest is about food. When my sisters were around fifteen years old Mama pushed them to start having sex because she hoped her daughters would catch someone who would bring food to the family, and fifteen was the age that Pygmies of her generation got married. She did not see this as a moral question. Like I said, everything in the forest is about food and everything you find belongs to you. This is how Mama thought. In providing for us she was a good mother because we were never hungry as kids.

Life in the forest is not stressful because there are no people around and stress is brought to you by other people. Happiness in the forest comes when you kill an antelope or if you catch some fish, because you know you will eat – and in Pygmy culture if you kill even one monkey everyone in the village will have a piece. There was also plenty of food in the forest: fruit, wild berries, mushrooms, edible leaves and roots, rodents such as mice, rats and squirrels, lizards, frogs, snakes, termites, caterpillars, larvae, worms and honey. Everything you find belongs to you, especially if you see it first. If we had plenty of meat we would look for other food and fruits before hunting animals again.

Pygmy children are taught how to hunt when they are young and when I was about six I learnt how to make a net. I collected a special type of liana and dried it. When it was dry I rolled it back and forth on my thigh to twist it. When I had many metres I made a net to catch forest rats. Like other kids I also made traps to catch birds that came to drink the nectar of a flower that lived along riverbanks. Most of our day was spent gathering food. Men hunted the big animals and women and children collected the fruit. When I was a child I was so happy when I found fruit and could eat a lot. If there was no fruit then we would go mushroom picking.

In the forest it is not so dark because there is little vegetation on the forest floor. Some light comes down through the canopy far above and you can see into the distance through the trees. We would look for tracks of antelope on the ground and for wild fruits. Wherever you go you can find *miteru*, a fruit shaped like a pear but smaller, which grows out of tree trunks near the ground. *Miteru* fruits are green but turn red when they are ripe, and are rich in vitamin C. People and monkeys both eat *miteru*, but they can never finish it all because there is so much. There is another fruit called *chambamba*, which is very sweet. The forest produces a lot and all the monkeys are satisfied and the humans as well. *Chambamba* is green but turns yellow when it is ripe. *Ngobya* is a small fruit with the same colour and taste as cherries. When you eat it, it makes your lips red and during the *ngobya* season it looks like everyone is wearing lipstick. *Embala* is another fruit, but you have to grill it on charcoals before you can eat it. Pygmies collect these fruits and sell them to people who live outside the forest, as well as eat it ourselves.

There were a lot of yams, which we prepare by washing then cooking in an earthenware pot. You have to take the skin off before you can eat them. You can buy yams in Australia, I think they are imported from Fiji, but they do not taste as good as those forest yams from Congo.

As well as fruit there were many kinds of mushrooms. Different mushrooms grow on different types of trees. *Mbumba* mushrooms grow on the misoki tree, and a mushroom called *bufloflo* grows on the *mifloflo* tree. Every morning we would pick *mbumba* mushrooms. These are very, very delicious mushrooms.

In the 1940s the Belgians started building the Kisangani–Bukavu road that ran through our forest. Pygmies did not want to work on it, so the Belgians forced people from elsewhere to come to the Bunyakiri area to do the work. One year Italians came to work on the road and they discovered our forest mushrooms. We have a story about two Italian men who had *mbumba* soup prepared for lunch. One of them, called something like Venundo, drank all the soup and didn't leave any for the second one. The one who missed out got angry and he started fighting with Venundo. They were punching each other! To see white people fighting over soup was really something for us. The people working for the Italians made up songs in KiTembo and Swahili about the fight over the *mbumba* soup. The Swahili version went something like this.

> *Venundo alikunywa supu akaacha nyama, akapigana na mwenzake.*
> *Venundo akasema nakubali tu uwane tu lakini siwezi kukuachia supu ya mbumba.*
> *Utamu ya mbumba inazidi yote!*

> Venundo drank the *mbumba* soup and ignored the meat.
> They fought with each other.
> Venundo said, 'I agree to fight, or to kill you, but I cannot leave the *mbumba* soup.
> The flavour of this soup is worth everything!'

When fruits were not in season there were some animals we could catch easily, such as *kapitwa*, a kind of rat. *Kapitwa* weigh up to 2 kilograms and are very tasty. Whenever we caught a *kapitwa*, I always wanted to eat it straightaway but it takes three to four days of smoking the meat before you can eat it. *Kapitwa* are so easy to catch. They live underground and we would search for the entrance to their tunnel and put a net over it. We would then look for a second hole – they always have two entrances – and put smoking sticks in it. The *kapitwa* would run out of the first hole and get caught in the net.

There were also lots of fish. We mostly fished by using a method called *kukiya*. This involves creating a channel around a small creek and diverting the water. As the small creek ran dry the fish would start to jump and we would catch them. Afterwards we would direct the water back to its natural course. We also used traps. We could put a trap in a creek in the afternoon and the next morning it would be full of fish and crabs. During the day we might go to find tortoises along streams.

We used to eat snake as well. There is one snake that is short and multicoloured and very poisonous if it bites you, but it tastes good. We also liked honey and the larvae of bees very much, but our favourite food was porcupine – this is the most delicious meat in the world. We had plenty of nice food in the forest!

You cannot kill a big animal if you are alone, so Pygmies always work together and hunt in a group. The way we fished – diverting the stream from its natural course – meant we also had to do this in a group. When we hunted monkeys, even little children participated. Everyone would clap their hands and make noises and throw things to get the monkeys to flee into a net. People close to the net would have knives or clubs and kill the monkeys before they ripped the nets apart and escaped. If there was a hunt for big animals, like antelope, children wouldn't participate because you have to follow the animal for a long distance. Only men did this, with dogs.

We also used nets to hunt small deer and wild pigs. Wild pigs are very dangerous and children were not allowed to come on pig hunts. Pigs defend themselves hard and if they catch you they will cut your arms and legs with their tusks. I remember a song about a man we knew, called Saenda, who went pig hunting. This song was very well known when I was a kid and tells of how Saenda was charged by a boar.

> *Era ngulube yakulaa Saenda lya lino ooo*
> *Ereee Saenda aeri reee.*
>
> We remember the pig that knocked out Saenda's teeth,
> Ohhh, Saenda has lost his teeth.

Saenda's song was sung in KiTembo because it was a small event and the song would have been composed by a Pygmy, but the song about Karanga's murder was sung in Swahili. When the Belgians started work on the road through our forest, people from many different ethnic groups were forced to live and work together and they spoke Swahili, which is spoken throughout East Africa and in Eastern Congo. The place where Karanga was murdered in the forest is not too far from the hut where the colonial Chief of Post lived and there would have been a road workers' camp nearby. A Swahili speaker from the camp probably composed Karanga's song.

Another dangerous animal Pygmies occasionally hunt is buffalo. To kill a buffalo we dig a hole about 3 metres deep across a forest path, then put light sticks over the top. We cover these with some soil and put leaves down so animals do not know there is a hole. Buffalo are not careful, so one might fall in and be unable to get out. Other buffalo will stay around until the one in the hole is dead or nearly dead. The Pygmies then come and kill it. Buffalo are not hunted with dogs because this is too dangerous; they would kill the dogs.

There is a strange animal that lives in the deep forest called the okapi. It looks a bit like a giraffe but has horizontal black and white stripes on its legs like a zebra. Our name for okapi is *ngenge* and this is the same word we use for zebra, but there are no zebras in our traditional country. Today okapi are only found in Northern Congo, but all the Pygmies in Eastern Congo know about the okapi and have stories and songs about them. I think the okapi must have been all around the Congo but got exterminated in the area I am from. Now, in Eastern Congo, the only traces of these animals are in songs. Mama used to sing a song about the legend of the *ngenge*, about how the singer killed one.

Pygmies occasionally killed elephants, but like buffalo this is not so easy. A group of men would put about ten spears in an elephant but it wouldn't die. It would continue to walk and the Pygmies would track it for one or two weeks until it died from its wounds. After the elephant finally died you had to cut it up into pieces then hang them over a smoky fire and dry the meat very slowly until it became hard and no insect could get inside. After this, the meat lasts for many months. I never went on a buffalo or elephant hunt because I left the forest before I became an adult.

Recently I was talking with Mama about when she lived in the forest before I was born. There was a gorilla that was coming to their camp and destroying their banana trees. Normally Pygmies do not hunt gorillas but this one was bothering them so they decided to kill it. They knew that gorillas were powerful animals. Mama said that if you do not have a brother with you, you should not try to hunt a gorilla because if it grabs you, it will smash you.

So that's another reason you need to hunt with your family: if you are hunting a dangerous animal it could fight back. If you hunt a gorilla with someone who is not a relative he will run away if it gets hold of you, but if you hunt with a brother he will try to stab the gorilla and carry you home if you are injured. Pygmies have an adage about this: 'If you are not related by blood, do not go hunting dangerous animals together.'

Dogs are important for hunting. Saenda, who had his teeth knocked out by the wild boar, had a special pig-hunting dog. My cousin Mito had a black-and-white hunting dog called Chimbemba. Chimbemba was smallish, because big dogs are no good in the forest. Hunting dogs are specially trained from when they are puppies and Chimbemba had been trained to catch *kapitwa* and *ngese*, a giant forest rat. A good hunting dog goes into the forest, catches something and brings it back, and Chimbemba did this. My family had a hunting dog specially trained to hunt baboons. These dogs are called *ngunda bioho* – 'baboon-hunting dog'. Baboons are very clever and baboon-hunting dogs have to be clever like the baboon to hunt it successfully. My younger brother, Buhavu, also had a hunting dog once. It was scared and lazy and if it saw an animal it would never attack, so Buhavu killed it with a machete.

In the forest we did not wear clothes because they would get snagged on branches. This would be a big problem if we were hunting because we had to move fast to follow animals. Both men and women were mostly naked except for what is called in French a *cache-sexe*: a small pouch that covered the sex, with string around the waist and through the legs to keep it in place. We all wore a *cache-sexe* when we were in the forest and for the men it made it a lot easier to run. Out of the forest we might put on a pair of shorts. When we saw someone had covered their whole body in clothes we would say they dressed like a rich person or a *muzungu*, a white man.

When Pygmies are on a hunt they use different techniques to make sure they don't get lost. If you go into an unfamiliar forest, such as when your hunting dogs are tracking an antelope, you might need to go twenty or thirty kilometres before you catch it. As they run through the forest following their dogs the hunters take a second to mark the trees with a machete as they pass. If you don't have a machete you can take some vegetation and tie it into a knot. Today, because of declining numbers of animals, hunters might have to walk for a day or two into the forest and make a small camp. You need to mark the path in order to get home. If someone becomes lost and does not return to the camp, people will fan out through the forest and make a special whistle with their fingers and their mouth. They will go to the top of a hill and whistle *katokorooo*, and the lost person can figure out where the sound is coming from.

Mama told me that the only real enemy of Pygmies in the forest was leopards. If Pygmies met a gorilla we would look at each other then each would go their own way. The same with chimpanzees – we would pass each other in the forest, minding our own business. Chimpanzees and gorillas were not harmful to us because they are not aggressive unless you approach their babies. We only started to eat them recently because of a lack of other meat, like antelope and monkey.

Pygmies were only scared of leopards. Because the walls of our huts are not strong and are only made of leaves, sometimes a leopard would pull sleeping people out and kill them. Mama told me about two or three people who were killed this way. One night the father-in-law of one of my relatives left his hut to go to the toilet, taking a burning stick with him to light the path. At night the forest is dark, and leopards are very silent. A leopard surprised him and jumped on him, scratching his face and chest. He had a *muuhu*, a traditional machete, and he fought back. Everyone in the camp woke up from the noise and rushed out to investigate. The leopard ran away but the man, although he lived, was left with many injuries.

4

Sang and danced and drank

Our days in the forest were spent gathering food but at night people would socialise. If it was not raining and there was moonlight we made a fire outside and sang and danced and drank. Pygmies drink banana wine, palm wine and alcohol made from fermented maize. In fact, we like any kind of alcohol. One of my aunts, one of Mama's sisters, loved alcohol. She never *sipped* wine – she would drink a whole gourd all at once. In KiTembo we have the word *otomera*, which means gulping down alcohol, or skol. We nicknamed this aunt 'Nabaotomera', which means 'auntie who skols'.

There are some dances that are unique to Pygmies, such as the *mutongo* and *kataronge*. Men, women and children would sing stories about love and do the *mutongo* and *kataronge* dances. The *mutongo* is a slow dance, but the *kataronge* is fast and you do small jumps. Men and women can do either dance as a couple. We sang while dancing, and even the people not dancing would sing. We also played instruments like tom-tom drums or the *likimbi*, the thumb piano, which is made of wood with eight metal strips fastened to it. The person playing it uses his thumbs to twang the metal strips. Sometimes *likimbis* are made from a small gourd because the hollow shape of the gourd can amplify the sound.

If we could not have a fire, such as when it was raining, we used candles for light. We made these out of the sap of a special tree. We cut the bark of the tree, collected the sap, waited until it hardened a bit and then rolled it into a candle shape. We did not have matches, but made fire using *mukore* wood. We put a small indent in a piece of *mukore* wood and held it between our toes. We then put a stick from a hardwood tree into the indentation and rubbed it quickly between our palms until it sparked and started burning dried leaves. If you used the right wood you could make fire in one or two minutes. If you had to use a different type of wood it would take much longer. People in the forest and countryside still use this method if they do not have matches or electricity.

When a Pygmy dies in the forest and we suspect bad spirits killed the person, then the same day everyone leaves that place and makes a new camp somewhere else. But not all spirits are bad. Nambacha was a Pygmy woman spirit who died a long time ago but continues to live in our forest. She was a very short woman. People would say they saw her looking for food in the forest or crabs in the river. If there is a Pygmy who is shorter than most, people say, 'Why are you short like Nambacha?' Everyone knows who they are talking about when this question is asked. Nambacha is not a harmful spirit. People out hunting might meet her, but she would always then just disappear.

When we want to remember someone who has died, we hold a *chioba* ceremony that might go for as long as a week, depending on the person who died and the person organising the ceremony. This does not have to happen right after the person has died. Someone might say, 'Let's make a *chioba* to remember Grandpa' for example, even if it is some years after he has died. When somebody dies their spirits go to the spirit world, and during the *chioba* people will dance to call the spirits of that person. When the dead person's spirits come they enter the dancers, who start to dance in an unusual way, and that is how we know the spirits have arrived.

Every few years when boys were the right age we might hold a hunting initiation ceremony for them. In fact, from four or five years old Pygmy children learn how to hunt, and by twelve boys might be going into the forest alone to hunt small deer, but the initiation ceremony means their skills are recognised. I remember going through the hunting ceremony. We were taken about half a kilometre away from our village in the forest, to a small temporary camp. We were taught how to hide in the forest when hunting, and how to crawl along the ground while fixing our eyes on prey at the same time. Someone went into the forest and hid, pretending to be an animal, and we hunted him down. After the training period there was a celebration. Some of the boys were dressed in layers and layers of leaves and long grasses that hung down from their head to the ground until they looked like a small bush. They would spin and jump and dance as they made their way back to the main camp followed by a whole crowd. Little children were scared of these dancing figures and ran away. As we came to the main camp everyone sang.

> The owner of the forest, comes from the forest
> The owner of the forest, comes from the forest
> The owner of the forest, comes from the forest
> Wild pig you shall kill
> Buffalo you shall kill
> Antelope you shall kill.

Traditionally, a second ceremony was held for boys after they had become recognised as hunters, when they were about fifteen. This was a circumcision ceremony, which can go for one or two months.

After the circumcision itself, boys would practise making traps, snares, nets and how to fish. In fact, a boy might already know how to hunt very well, but if you are not circumcised it is very difficult to get a wife because girls do not want to marry you, so all boys get circumcised. During the ceremony the selected boys are taken a short distance from the main camp. The other children know where they are and visit them to see what is going on. The boys' bodies are painted with white clay and red clay, and sometimes when I was a kid we were allowed to put the dots on their arms and chests or the stripes on their faces. During circumcision they use the *molimo*, which is a kind of long trumpet. Kimbirikiti is like a god of circumcision for Pygmies and Bantu, and they say that when the *molimo* makes sound it is Kimbirikiti talking. When this happens women need to lock themselves in their huts so they cannot see the *molimo*, otherwise they will go blind and die. But the people who said this are just lying – nothing happens to the women and the sounds from the *molimo* are just sounds made by the person blowing into it.

We do not all go through the forest ritual. I was circumcised when I was at a mission school. I still remember how it hurt! Papa would have liked me to go through the forest ritual but the school principal said it was a pagan practice so I did not go.

Circumcision used to be done using a piece of bark from a special bamboo tree that when peeled off was very sharp. Juice from another plant was put on the wound to dry the blood. For about two months after the ceremony the newly circumcised boys would wash in the river in the morning. The cold water helped the wound heal. Now we use razors from China and put penicillin powder on the wound.

Little boys are afraid of circumcision so the adults used to tell us a story to persuade us to go through with it. They told us that in the forest there was a beautiful lady called Nangera, and that all you needed to do was put your penis inside her and when you took it out you were circumcised! They wanted to make it sound easy, but I knew it was a myth.

We had a song about circumcision, about a boy called Ndoole.

Ndoole alilir'obwali,
Eeh, utenda waliliri r'obwali bwao,
Eeh, utenda waliliri r'obwali bwetfu

Ndoole cries because of circumcision,
Eeh, do not cry for your circumcision,
Eeh, never cry for our circumcision.

Being circumcised was a sign that a boy could make his own traps, hunt his own animals and get married. He was grown up. Pygmies still carry out the circumcision ritual, even though the Catholics and Protestants told us it was a pagan ceremony.

If there was no ceremony or dance in our camp at night then we stayed in our huts and the old women told stories. Not stories about real people, but fables to educate young people and to teach values. I remember one of these fables about a girl who didn't want to get married. Whenever a boy came to make friends with her, she refused him. Time passed and a very smart and good boy came along and the girl told herself, 'This is the right one'. They went off together into the forest, but when they were alone the boy vanished into a tree. He was actually a spirit and not a human being at all.

The moral of the story is that girls wanting to get married should not wait for the perfect boy, because he is just a fantasy and does not exist.

5

That's what I think of Pygmies

In 1969, another construction company arrived to do work on the road through our forest. Papa worked as a labourer for the company for about a year. The company then won a contract to build an airport at Kavumu, near Lake Kivu. Dad went there hoping to get more work with them but he was unsuccessful. However, he met a Bantu man, Mr Lulanga, who was from the Shi tribe and had a plot of land where he grew bananas, cassava and beans, and Papa went to work for him. Our home was in a banana grove about fifty metres away from Mr Lulanga's house, out of sight. Mama and Papa built a hut just like we had in the forest. Papa looked after Mr Lulanga's crops and got paid in food and banana wine, and Mama was given old clothes by Mr Lulanga's wife.

Mr Lulanga's children went to the local school, the Kabuga Protestant Primary School. I was eight years old and it bothered me that all the children of my age went to school but I stayed at home, feeling lonely. I pestered my parents to send me to school, not realising that going to school was costly and that my parents were too poor to afford school fees. Finally my persistence convinced my parents that I was serious and I enrolled in Year 1. One of Mr Lulanga's sons, who was in Year 4, gave me his old school shirt and shorts. The uniform was far too big, and because I did not have a belt I used a cord made from dried banana leaf to keep my pants up.

The Kabuga school was an orderly mission school, with brick walls painted white and desks and chairs in neat rows. Norwegian and Swedish missionaries ran the school but the teachers were Congolese, mostly from the Shi tribe. There were six levels at the school and I started in the lowest grade, the one for little kids. My class had about fifty pupils, forty boys and perhaps ten girls. There were no other BaTembo or Pygmy children. I was the only one.

School was from eight in the morning until three in the afternoon. It was a 4-kilometre walk from home that took about an hour. I used to walk there every morning with the son of Papa's master, passing through banana farms along a dirt path until we got to the road. We then followed the road and had to cross the Kavumu marketplace and shops in the town centre to reach the school. The town centre was always interesting. Women would be selling peanuts, bananas and avocados, and school children with money would buy a snack on the way home from school.

I first became aware of politics when I was at this school, because every morning we had to stand in assembly and sing praises to our president, Joseph Mobutu. The government forced shops to put up President Mobutu's picture and some people even had a picture of Mobutu in their homes, although we didn't in our hut made of sticks and leaves. I still remember the picture: Mobutu wore black-framed glasses and a spotted leopard-skin cap. Mama and Papa knew about Mobutu but were not interested in politics and paid no attention to any of it.

I had some good friends at that school. There was Ombeni, who didn't care that I was a BaTembo or a Pygmy. Little kids don't care about that sort of thing. And Zachary. His dad was rich and owned a truck, and Zachary wore shoes. Zachary's house was in the shape of a rectangle, was made of wood and had a tin roof. Most houses were round and had a thatched roof. Our own home just had leaves and grass everywhere.

My teacher at the school was Mr Enoch. 'Which tribe are you from?' he asked me, as all the other students in the whole school were Shi. I told him 'BaTembo'. 'That,' he replied, 'means you are a Pygmy.' I told him no, just BaTembo. Mr Enoch despised me. He made a point of calling me a 'Pygmy' in a way that told the other students I was inferior. The fact that I was dressed in an old uniform with holes in the pants attracted the attention of all the students in my class, and the whole school. Mr Enoch drew attention to my uniform in front of the other children and warned me many times to come with a new one, but my parents could not afford it. They could barely afford the school fees, which cost 2 makutas, or about $2, per term. One day I failed to do a task and Mr Enoch whipped me. I bled from the nose and from where the whip had cut me. The school principal and other teachers were upset with him, and many students felt pity for me, but it didn't change Mr Enoch's behaviour.

There is a song I remember from primary school, a really discriminatory song that people sang to taunt us.

> *Babiri kuta, o murhembo kazi bo buhiri n'omurhwakazi go mulambizo.*
>
> Two women for a makuta and one Tembo woman as a bonus, plus one Pygmy woman to be a doormat.

What it means is that two Bantu women were worth a makuta but a worthless BaTembo woman could be thrown in as a bonus … and then the buyer would get a Pygmy woman as a second bonus to wipe their dirty feet on. People still sing this song today, but Bantu BaTembo do not sing it because it insults them as well.

After three months at the Kabuga school I had a very bad experience. One day I wet my pants, and Mr Enoch hit me very hard with his fists and kicked me. Mr Enoch shouted, 'That's what I think of Pygmies!' as he punched me in front of the other kids. I remember bleeding from my ears and nose. The principal and the other teachers were angry with Mr Enoch, and they told the son of Papa's Bantu master to take me home.

My parents were not surprised to see me beaten half-dead by my teacher. They had told us that Bantu always treat Pygmies badly. But I did not understand Mr Enoch when he told me that Pygmies are not human! On Monsieur Vandeward's plantation and Mr Lulanga's farm I was used to seeing people from many different backgrounds, with different skin colours, with a body similar to mine: made up of a head, neck, torso, two arms and two legs, walking like us, and eating similar food to ours. At that age, I could not comprehend discrimination and racism.

After I arrived home my body started to swell up. My parents massaged me with hot water and herbs from the forest. People told my parents to complain to the police, but complaining was costly. The police asked my parents to pay 5 makutas – what they called the 'arrest fee' – to arrest Mr Enoch, but where could my parents find 5 makutas? They could barely pay the school fees. I got better but my parents stopped me from going back to school. I myself was scared to go back in case I got beaten again. 'Will you insist on going to school again?' Papa asked. 'No,' I told him. 'I won't insist.'

'School is not for us. Now you see for yourself why we didn't go to school.'

My parents decided the only way to get justice, to be treated fairly, was to run away from those people. We decided to move closer to the Kahuzi forest where there were more BaTembo, and Papa found a job on another Belgian-owned plantation. Mr Lulanga's family was upset to see us go. Not because they liked us, but because they were losing their cheap labour.

6

A mouse cannot give birth to a rat

We called our new home 'Mr François' Farm' because it was looked after by a Belgian man called Mr François, but the plantation didn't actually belong to him. Mr François was the manager and looked after the tea factory and cinchona crop for the owner, who was absent. Mr François preferred to work with Bantu than with Pygmies, because Bantu were more stable. Pygmies would work for a week and then just go off into the forest to make charcoal or to hunt. Most of the workers on the farm were Tutsis from Rwanda who had fled into Congo in the 1960s to escape persecution by the Hutu-dominated government there. The rest were Bantu from the Shi and Havu tribes, and there were also some Pygmies, including our family, who lived and worked on the farm when it suited us.

The camp where the Pygmies lived was right on the edge of Mr François' farm, next to the Kahuzi-Biéga National Park. The government authorities wanted the camp moved off the boundary because they suspected us of hunting in the forest. They were right. Pygmies are not farmers, so Dad wasn't really interested in looking after livestock or tending crops. Meat was expensive and my father was not rich enough to have chickens or goats, so if we wanted meat we had to hunt for it. All Papa thought about was going back into the forest to check his snares when he was finished work for the day. Or if he was out amongst the tea bushes and heard a monkey in the forest, he would think about how he could catch that monkey after work. In the rainy season, when there were a lot of animals around and they were easy to trap, Papa and the other Pygmies living in the camp would desert the farm for up to three months to hunt. They would semi-dry the meat then come home to eat some or to sell or exchange it for other food.

The authorities knew that Pygmies and other hunters poached game in the Kahuzi-Biéga reserve and used to stop and search them when they were walking into town if they looked suspicious. If authorities caught a man with bush meat he would be fined, but they never stopped children so a few times I used to take meat to sell in town. I would hide it in a bag and never got stopped.

Mama developed a strategy to get Papa out of trouble when he was caught poaching. She discovered that the local territorial administrator, Salumu, liked monkey, so several times Mama smoked monkey or antelope meat and gave it to him for free. He always asked if anyone had seen us come to him, and when we said no he would take it. When Papa was caught, Salumu would then let him off with a warning. People in other countries like Kenya, Rwanda and Burundi do not eat monkey, but Congolese like monkey. In fact, we eat everything. This is why all the laws about hunting in national parks in Congo do not get much respect. But these laws, from the time of the Belgians, changed the way Pygmies could hunt: if we were caught with a net or a lance we could be put in prison, so we switched to using small traps and snares that we did not have to carry around.

When we were growing up on Mr François' farm, if we had no food Mama would take her machete, walk into the jungle and after one or two hours bring home something to eat. She was very skilled at finding herbs and wild yams. Every morning at five or six o'clock she woke up to go the river to check her traps, and by 7 am we would be eating fish or crabs. On some mornings, around four o'clock while everyone else was still sleeping, she used to visit the farms of Bantu villagers and bring home to us their cassava and bananas. In Congo we have a saying, 'You reap what you sow,' but in KiTembo we have another saying: 'Pygmies reap what they don't sow.'

Mama also went secretly into the national park to collect firewood. She used to sell it to Bantus or exchange it for food. Once she was bargaining with a Bantu man and he offered her so little money for the firewood that she refused completely. He got angry that she had refused, took the wood, kept his money and hit her. 'Go and complain now!' he said. Mama returned crying to the Pygmy camp. Someone told her to take the man to the local court, and with a group of people she went and found him. A crowd gathered and a Bantu *mwami* got involved. The man told the *mwami*: 'This Pygmy woman is very impolite. I gave her the money and she returned it, saying she wanted to sell the wood to someone else. I got angry and slapped her and kept my money and the wood to punish her.' The *mwami* told Mama that her wood was illegally cut from the national park anyway, and he supported the man who had hit Mama. But he also told the man to give Mama some money. The man said he did not have any but would pay her later. Mama never got the money.

When Bantu cheat Pygmies or refuse to honour a promise of payment, they do not want the Pygmies to react badly. For example, most Pygmies work at times on the farms of Bantu villagers. The villager might promise to give them two or three measures of beans as payment, but then only give them one. Bantu have a saying, 'Don't get upset like a Pygmy.' What they mean is the Pygmy should calm down and not be so upset. Bantu say this because Pygmies hate being cheated or patronised – and we can tell when it is happening – and react badly. We will just leave and walk away and refuse to have anything to do with them, like when Mama refused to sell the Bantu man her firewood. Then *he* got angry.

Mama told me this story about the firewood because she worries about me writing this book and does not support it. She thinks talking about the way Pygmies have been treated is complaining, and that complaining is useless. Instead of getting better, things get worse. She says, 'You have to be careful, my son, of saying you have been treated badly. You only get treated equally if you are dealing with another poor person. If you have a problem with someone who is not poor, you will never be treated equally.' It's true. There are Pygmies who have had their lands sold to Bantu. If we complain, the territorial administrator or the lawyers will be given a cow by the person who bought the land, and because they have been bought off, they do nothing for the Pygmies.

White people with the power to help also ignored us. This was the case with the Pygmies who were thrown out of the Kahuzi-Biéga National Park that was created in part of our traditional country, and which is now a UNESCO World Heritage Site. The headquarters of the park is called Madaga. This is the name of a Pygmy family that is still living. Namadaga, who was pregnant with twins and was speared by Grandpa Kasasa, was a daughter of this family. The Madaga family's land, their area of hunting, became part of the national park. So much money is given to support the park but the Madaga family is living in poverty. 'Look,' Mama told me, 'the white people who made the park never did anything to help the Madaga family. Monsieur Vandeward also took land from the forest and made a farm. He employed some Pygmies, but Bantu had the top positions and he did not send any Pygmies to school.'

It is not just the Pygmies who are discriminated against – all BaTembo are. The BaTembo are no more than 10 per cent Pygmy, about 50 per cent Bantu and 40 per cent Pygmoid – people who are half-half, or mixed with Bantu – but people from the neighbouring Shi and Havu tribes do not make these distinctions. 'Whoever has Pygmy blood is a Pygmy,' they say. They have another saying: 'A small smelly mouse cannot give birth to a rat.' In other words, the Pygmy is the small smelly mouse and the rat – something good and delicious in Congo – is the Bantu. They think there is no way someone with Pygmy ancestry can become a Bantu.

Many Bantu and Pygmoid BaTembo are offended when they are called Pygmies. They may be proud of being Bantu for the reason that their ancestor, Katembo, was a Bantu, or they may even not know their origin, or they may just want to ignore it. They try to erase anything to do with Pygmies. Some BaTembo *mwami* are Pygmoid but they say they are Bantu even though they originate from Pygmy mothers. Educated BaTembo, whether Bantu, Pygmoid or Pygmy, do not even want to talk about being BaTembo due to the discrimination and negative stereotype that surrounds our origin.

All BaTembo, including Pygmy BaTembo, want independence from other Bantu tribes. Since Congo's independence we have wanted recognition as a distinct and separate tribe. There is a concentration of BaTembo in the Bunyakiri area, but most BaTembo are sprinkled across the chiefdoms of other tribes and don't dominate any one region. In all these territories Pygmies, and BaTembo, are subjected to the authority of the *mwami* from other tribes. This subjugation has caused us humiliation and marginalisation. We find it unacceptable to cohabit with tribes who consider us primitive and backward because of our Pygmy ancestry, but we must.

There is also discrimination within the Pygmy community. For example, we say there are three kinds of Pygmy. The first we call *BaTwa be Bungukuma* in KiTembo. This means something like 'stocky Pygmies with muscular bodies'. They are shorter than normal Pygmies, they are strong – their chests are like hard stones – and their whole body works together perfectly. This kind of Pygmy is quite hairy and they don't like to mix with other people. The second kind is a normal Pygmy, like my family. Once Mama got some pork from a Bantu man and promised to pay him back in a few weeks with firewood. She was late giving him the wood and he started to say bad things about Pygmies. Mama got upset and told him, 'We were not like the *BaTwa be Bungukuma*. We are normal Pygmies.' What she meant is that we were better than the *BaTwa be Bungukuma*, because they would never pay him back but she eventually would. The third kind of Pygmy is the Pygmoid people. Amongst these three kinds of Pygmies there are those who are poor, those who have an average life, the honest and the dishonest.

Some of this discrimination by Pygmies is an attempt to improve their living standards. If a full-blood Pygmy has the opportunity to get some money, he wants to use it to marry a Bantu woman to improve his status. If a Pygmy woman is married to a Bantu it is lucky for her because her status will also go up. Full-blood Pygmies are sometimes scared of Pygmoid people, because Pygmoid people see themselves as masters of the full-bloods and act like this towards us.

But Pygmies are very accepting of being ruled and pushed around. When Bantu were taking our land in the Bunyakiri area, they told the Pygmies, 'We took your land.' The Pygmies simply repeated an adage: '*Chitaka chitalya boshi-munalyaa.*' 'We can't all be rulers: let those who are rulers, rule.'

7

American witchcraft

I went back to school when we moved to Mr François' farm. Because Papa was working for white people and because he spoke Swahili, he was seen as more sophisticated and civilised – certainly much more than other Pygmies. I felt that I was too, and it gave me courage to go back to school, even though my parents never encouraged me to do this. However, all the other children on the farm went to school and one of the farm managers said that Pygmy children should go as well. 'Just go,' said Mama and Papa but they never showed any interest. Even now, no-one else in my family has been to school. My brothers and cousins just got a dog and a spear to go hunting, and that was it.

Mr François was a kind man. He was tall and thin, and put oil in his hair to make it sit perfectly. He used to give me lifts in his dark blue Peugeot 404 from his farm to his office, and then I walked the rest of the way to the local school. Mr François left for work early so I had to get up early every morning if I wanted a lift. No other Pygmy ever stepped inside that car. He knew I was from the Pygmy camp and occasionally he gave me 2 or 3 makutas to buy something, but I would use it to pay my school fees. This amount was nothing to him, but sometimes it paid my fees for an entire term. Papa was not interested in paying for my education, but Mr François' servants told him that if a white man was helping a Pygmy boy to go to school, that boy must be smart. They encouraged Dad to pay my fees and he eventually decided to contribute.

As a boy I wanted Mr François to like me and I used to think about how I could get his affection. I decided that if I got up early and was always waiting outside his house for a lift to school this would impress him. I think it worked because Mr François only ever gave me a lift. Occasionally if I was with one or two other boys I would wave to him hoping he would stop, but he never did if I was not alone. During my rides with Mr François he asked me about school. 'Who is your teacher? What did you study today?' He did not speak Swahili so we spoke in French. He asked simple questions because he knew I did not speak French very well, although I had started learning it in school. Over time these conversations improved my French a lot. I was proud of being able to talk to him and that I rode in his car. I asked him about his wife and children, and when they were going to visit the farm. They lived in Europe, so perhaps he missed them and showed kindness to me because of that. His children visited in the school holidays. They were so clean and white. I would greet them with, '*Bonjour. Ça va?*' but they were teenagers and did not have much time for me. I knew I was inferior to them.

When I was ten, one of the Belgian employees from the farm moved to the city of Bukavu and took his Congolese cook with him. I was friends with one of the cook's sons, Raimond. During the school holidays I asked Mr François if he would take me to Bukavu the next time he went so I could see Raimond. He did! We drove together, just the two of us, in his car. I sat in the front with my bare feet, and we spoke in French. Pygmies in the camp said, 'The white man will eat him or sell his blood!', but the fact that Mr François had been giving me lifts to school meant my parents and I were not afraid. I was in Bukavu for two weeks and it was my first time in a city. I saw lights everywhere at night, including along the streets, and the buildings were all very tall.

From about this age I started to have a double life. Like other Pygmies on the farm, Papa worked when he wanted to but he also went hunting back in the forest when he wanted to, and sometimes I would go with him. I was comfortable in the Pygmy camp and in the forest, but I also started to become familiar with Mr François' life – with modern life: cars and electricity and French language and the tea factory. I was not living a modern life but I could see it and it started to become normal for me and was no longer strange. Other Pygmies never went near Mr François' house. There was no roadblock but they were scared because Mr François' servants would chase them away. The servants did not chase me because they knew Mr François was friendly towards me and gave me lifts to school. When Mr François' children walked to the Pygmy camp where we lived, everyone hid in their huts or in the forest because they were afraid. But I was different. I wasn't afraid. I had lost my fear of white men because of Mr François. I realised he was kind, and just a person like me.

I went to school regularly for the years we lived on Mr François' farm. One year, when I was in about Year 4, Grandma Nabikusa and Uncle Simon, Mama's half-brother, visited us from Bunyakiri. Mama told them that I spoke French with a white man and Uncle Simon could not believe it. 'I'm going to send my son to school as well!' he said. Uncle Simon told me what a big and busy place Bunyakiri was, and said that there were many other schools there. He proposed that I come and live with Grandma Nabikusa in Bunyakiri. I think Uncle Simon wanted to show me off to his neighbourhood, to show them that his nephew, a Pygmy boy, could speak French like white people. It is normal in Congo for children to go and live with aunties or uncles, so my parents thought this was no problem and I went to Bunyakiri.

In Bunyakiri I attended a couple of different schools, including a Pentecostal school. At the Pentecostal school top-ranked students were given gifts as rewards and encouragement, and I always came second in class. Two terms in a row I received a pair of shorts as a prize. The boy who came first went on to work for the United Nations in Haiti and Côte d'Ivoire.

I lived with Grandma Nabikusa and her younger sister, Namukonzi, on the outskirts of Bunyakiri. They had a small one-room house with a thatched roof and walls made of a lattice of sticks with mud smoothed over the outside. Grandma did not have any blankets. She used sheep hides instead, and used to cover me with two or three at night to keep me warm. I remember this home well. We were the poorest in the neighbourhood and it was in that house that I ate cat for the first time. We had not eaten meat for a while when a Bantu gave us a cat. Bantu do not eat cat, so if they caught one, or had a dead one, they might give it to Grandma. Grandma killed the cat, put it on a fire to burn off the hair then cut it into pieces and put it in a pot with salt, water and a bit of oil. When we got that cat it was like a big party.

Grandma Nabikusa eventually left Bunyakiri to go back to the forest, so after two years I moved back to Mr François' farm where I attended the local Kasheke Institute for Years 7 and 8. The Kasheke Institute was run by Baptist missionaries from the United States. It was too far from the farm to travel to every day so I stayed in the school's dormitory.

In my first year, there were about ten of us from the Pygmy

camp who went to school but each year the number of Pygmy children enrolled decreased. In the end there was only one other Pygmy boy still at school with me. All the others had gone back to the forest. Most of the children at the school were from the Shi or Havu tribes. There were wooden desks in each classroom, the kind with bench seats and a top that lifted up to show a space underneath for books. We had to sit in pairs but the other kids refused to sit with us. 'If we sit with a Pygmy we will get sick,' they would say. The Shi and Havu boys were poor but we Pygmies were even poorer and they did not want to mix with us. The school's principal defended us. He was upset when other boys refused to sit with us and he forced them to share a desk. However, the principal and teachers discouraged us from doing some traditional practices, saying they were against the teachings of the Bible.

I was bullied over one incident in particular. The American missionary who ran the school was Mr Pearce. He taught religion. One day he announced that he was returning to the United States for good. He had two horses, two cats and two dogs, and needed to do something with them before he left. In Congo we don't have horses and we were amazed that one of the horses had been given a name, Bun, and even more amazed that it came to Mr Pearce when he called 'Bun! Bun!' People said, 'These white people came here to teach us religion, but they are mysterious people!' Others said that Mr Pearce must have good witchcraft that he could talk to animals. Mr Pearce knew that everyone was poor and could not afford to feed his pets. He did not want the animals to suffer, so he shot the horses and the dogs.

As for his cats, I had noticed they were very spoilt. Well fed. I asked Mr Pearce if I could have them and when he left he gave them to me. I took them to the dormitory kitchen and cooked them the way Grandma had shown me. The other kids stood around calling me names. I offered them some cooked cat but they refused. I complained to the dormitory supervisor and he tried to punish the kids who were taunting me, but they kept doing it.

In Years 7 and 8 we were taught English by Miss Foss, an old American lady with lots of curly white hair, who laughed and joked a lot. Miss Foss loved science and technology, and we heard about rockets and space, and Armstrong and the Apollo 11 mission. Miss Foss showed us pictures of rockets and explained how they were much more powerful than aeroplanes and could go into space. And she told us about the United States, about Martin Luther King and how he was killed fighting for the rights of black people. She explained that black people went to America as slaves but were now free. She said everyone in America could afford to buy a small car. We didn't really think she would lie to us, but we found that hard to comprehend and we knew then that every American must be rich. Even where we lived in Congo the only people with cars, other than Belgian settlers, were Americans: Mr Pearce and Miss Foss herself. She had a small Volkswagen. Rich Congolese in our area had bicycles. We asked her if black people in America could also afford cars and she said, 'Yes'. She also told us about infrastructure. She said that in America every house can be reached by a car driving along a road. That amazed us. We could not imagine there was such a place on this Earth! When she told us about Armstrong going to the moon we thought how powerful Americans' witchcraft must be to get them there. Much stronger than African witchcraft.

Outside of Miss Foss' English classes we were forced to speak

French at school. If I spoke Swahili I would be beaten. Not by Mr Pearce: he was too high up and just taught religion. It was the Congolese teachers who beat us. At lunchtime the teachers played a kind of game. They carried a cow bone and if they heard any student say just one word in Swahili or the Shi language, that student had to carry the bone. You only got beaten if you said whole sentences in those languages, so there was a lot of broken French spoken. I had an advantage over other students because of my conversations with Mr François, but I also had my turn carrying the cow bone.

Eventually switching from one language to another came automatically to me. What motivated me to learn more languages when I was growing up was that if I only spoke KiTembo I would be identified as a Pygmy or, if someone respected me, as a BaTembo. Speaking it was not a choice for me; it was the language I was born into and everyone in the surrounding population looked down on me as a result. Because it was not a choice, I did not like speaking it. All the Pygmies outside the forest try to change their habits, including the way they dress and their way of talking. BaTembo need to speak the language of powerful tribes around them so they can assimilate into that tribe. This was not just about copying others, but *becoming* others. Speaking KiTembo immediately revealed me to others.

About 70 per cent of the workers on Mr François' farm were refugees from Rwanda, Tutsis mostly. They spoke Kinyarwanda and I learnt this language from them and their children. We used to speak Kinyarwanda on our way to and from school, and I sang their songs. There was also a small number of Hunde people on Mr François' farm. Whenever we interacted with them they behaved in a superior way. Katembo, the ancestor of all the BaTembo, was a Hunde himself, but Hunde think all BaTembo are Pygmies or Pygmoids. They look down on the KiTembo language because it is like bad Hunde, a pidgin, but they can understand us and we can understand them.

Shi is the biggest tribe in the northern part of South Kivu, so I was surrounded by the Shi language. Shi speak their language with pride because they are proud of their origins. They are descended from Mwami Kabari, who was the King of Kabari many centuries ago. They also feel proud when others learn their language. It is not like this for BaTembo Pygmies. No-one wants to learn KiTembo! We even try to avoid our own language because if we speak it then immediately people think we are lower class.

To be counted as a civilised person in my part of Congo it is essential to speak Swahili, which is spoken in Congo because when the Arabs were trading slaves from Central Africa they imposed this language on people. It is spoken across East Africa and Eastern Congo. However, people from Kinshasa, the capital city over in the west of Congo, speak Lingala. President Mobutu, our president from 1965 to 1997, made his speeches in it and popular music is in Lingala, so if you don't speak this language it means you come from the bush.

But in Congo educated people speak French. If you speak French you are on top and feel superior to those speaking Swahili or Shi, so at school I concentrated a lot on learning French. It is the language that I definitely find most pleasurable to speak. Seventeenth- and eighteenth-century writers made French very sweet. When I was learning French and reading authors like Boileau, Molière, La Fontaine and Saint-Exupéry, I felt that French was a language that had come from Heaven. I wanted to speak like those writers! The Baptists at the Kasheke Institute introduced me to the Bible and it made me think about what I believed. The beliefs I had traditionally – what I had learnt from my parents – were in conflict with what I was learning in religious studies, but also in science class. I became confused by everything I was learning about religion. I didn't know what to believe. This conflict between traditional beliefs, religious belief and science pushed me to study and try to find where the truth lay.

In school and in church, whenever someone taught me something I always wanted to know the facts, the truth. I am naturally analytical and with anything I was able to think about, whether scientific, philosophical or religious, I tried to find some proof before reaching my own conclusion. What I found was that traditional beliefs were just imagination and were used to make people scared, but I realised the majority of people believe in these things. For example, whether Congolese are educated or not, most believe deaths are caused by witches. They don't believe in heart attacks, for example. In Congo if someone dies, such as your child, you go to a pastor who will fast and then pray to God, who then reveals to the pastor what happened. You might have to fast and pray with him, and there might be a revelation from God that an aunt, an uncle or a neighbour killed the child. In Congo pastors are responsible for killing lots of people by saying that they have been inspired by God to say that the person is a witch, and then telling the village – 'In name of Jesus!' – that the person should be killed.

I thought people were being misled. I could not follow the majority because I thought they were going the wrong way, for example in believing that spirits live in the forest. The Baptists were teaching something similar to Pygmies' beliefs: that you have a spirit and if you die it goes to a certain place. Both Pygmies and Bantu believe spirits live in the forest. Pygmies do the *chioba* ceremony to venerate the dead and to appease their spirits, so the spirits won't harm the living, but I did not understand why those spirits of dead people never helped their families. I concluded that it was because the spirits could not harm or help anyone because there was no such thing. When I was in high school I studied science, microbiology. I learnt about the composition of the human body, which has been proved scientifically to be composed of water, oxygen and minerals – in millions of cells. When oxygen leaves the body, everything stops working and this is death. It is like when you hit a pigeon in the street with your car – the pigeon isn't going to live somewhere else, like Heaven. It's dead. I know there is a god and that Satan exists, but I stopped believing in spirits, Heaven or Hell. Praying to the dead or praying that somebody will go to Heaven is useless, scientifically. I have not seen proof that praying works, so to pray to spirits or to give respect to the spirits of the dead – like to Nambacha, the female spirit that Pygmies say they sometimes see when they are gathering food in the forest – is like giving respect to … a cup. Cups are inert material. A cup doesn't know if you are respecting it or not.

Religious studies was compulsory at the Baptist school. You needed 50 per cent to pass each subject and you had to pass religious studies to continue to the next grade. This made me very motivated to study religion, but all my study had a different effect to what the school wanted. I asked my religious studies teacher, Mr Lazar, questions about religion and pointed out that what we were learning in class – about people going to Hell – seemed contradictory to what I understood God said in Genesis. I was sure Genesis said people who disobeyed God would return to where they came from, and to me that meant to dust, decomposition, not Hell. Mr Lazar was nice to me but he wanted me to believe whatever he taught. When I pointed out these contradictions he became angry. 'Why are you asking this question?! You have to follow what I am teaching!' A light switched on for me when that happened. I realised that however we venerate the dead, or their spirits, the dead are not conscious of it and are not even in pain. They are just decomposing. As for the living, they say this stuff to make people scared and to have authority over them. It is false teaching. But in the Religious studies exam there was a question about what happens to sinners. I wrote: 'They will go to Hell.' I had to, to pass.

The Baptists and Catholics also teach that you can solve problems by praying. I did not believe in this either. There are many problems in life that are in the hands of those who have power. They are the ones who can solve the problem. For example, when there is war in Congo, which is often, Congolese say, 'Let's get together and pray for peace!' People have been praying for peace for years and it has not worked yet. It is like going to a priest to get rid of worms in your stomach. Worms don't leave unless you take medication. Or malaria – it is mosquitoes that put the malaria parasite in your blood. You need to take something to kill the parasite, not pray.

8

A miracle hen

After finishing middle school at the Kasheke Institute I wanted to continue to Year 9 at high school. My family didn't have any money and my parents were not interested in my education. However, there was an old primary school teacher of mine, Mr Katipula, who really loved me. He gave me a big, beautiful white hen that turned out to be a miracle hen. After about two weeks she started to lay eggs. She laid all these eggs and hatched out 23 chicks. She then laid another 25 eggs and from these 24 chicks hatched. In two goes I had gone from having one hen to more than 40 chickens.

Mama and Papa started to eat my chickens. Pygmies don't farm. They don't keep goats or cattle or chickens, they just kill and eat, kill and eat, so Mum and Dad were not going to wait to collect eggs each day. They just ate one of my chickens when they wanted meat. I knew I was going to lose all my chickens, so I took about twenty-five to the market and sold them. I decided to use the money I got to pay for high school. I talked to a friend, Benoît, who was already in high school in Bukavu, about what I should do. He was from a wealthy family and they had an empty house in Bukavu. He suggested I go to school there, like him, and that we live together. I used my money from the chickens to travel to Bukavu to sit the entry exam to attend the Bagira Institute, a local high school. Everything depended on me passing that exam, and I did.

I went back to Bunyakiri but I needed to raise more money to buy a uniform and to pay school fees. I could only rely on my chickens but my parents were big predators and whenever they needed meat they killed one. I decided I had to sell my remaining chickens. I had to do it quickly before all my chickens were eaten, leaving me with no assets. I told my parents to care for the miracle hen and three other chickens, and sold the rest.

With the money I bought a white shirt, blue trousers and a pair of black shoes, and in September 1978 I started Year 9 at the Bagira Institute. Benoît and I moved into his family's empty house, but eventually this became a problem. Benoît was from a wealthy family and he had a lot of money. He was about 22, five years older than me, and was in Year 11. It is common for older people to be in school in Congo, because whether they continue to the next level depends on whether they pass their exams and whether they can pay school fees. Benoît was not stupid but he was lazy and missed a lot of school so did not advance quickly. He had a lot of pride, although not about school. He had pocket money, changed girlfriends daily, and he could buy beer and go to bars. He was bringing girlfriends to the house when I was trying to sleep. I would hear them having sex at two or three o'clock in the morning, drunk. He would then miss school for a couple of days, but because the teachers were poor he gave them money to pass him if he failed a test. He had a better standard of living than the teachers so he could easily bribe them.

Benoît and I had agreed that I would contribute to bringing food and paying rent, but most of the time I was unable to do this and Benoît let me live with him out of mercy. But he didn't show me respect. When he went out to bars he never invited me – I wasn't worthy enough to go with him. Normally in Congo people will invite you to a bar if they think you might invite them next time.

However, if they think you don't have any money they won't invite you. They pretend it is about friendship, but it's about reciprocity and Benoît stopped pretending. My memories of Mr François and Mr Katipula encouraged me to continue to go to school, but I wanted to leave Benoît. However, I was like his servant, with nowhere else to go and no financial means to leave him.

At the Bagira Institute there was a teacher, Professor Job, who had been a Catholic priest. A Grand Seminarian. As a priest he had started to question Catholic teachings. He said the idea of punishment for sins in an eternal fire was not in the Bible but was made up by priests and traditional churches in Europe and Israel to make people scared. He got kicked out of the seminary because he refused to stop saying such things. In Congo Catholic priests have a very high standard of living with many privileges. He left all this – the priesthood, the seminary – to became a Jehovah's Witness. They don't believe in Hell or eternal punishment. He also got married and had children.

Everyone at the Bagira Institute knew about Professor Job's background. He taught Philosophy and French to Years 10, 11 and 12. When you looked at him you could tell he was an intelligent thinker. He was in his thirties, tall and clean-cut with clear brown skin and he always dressed very chic. Some students and teachers called him 'Mr Socrates' and others would say, 'No, no, he's Mr Plato!' In his classes he emphasised thinking and theory. He taught us that we have to question any theory, and to ask: 'Why has this theory been developed? Why does it exist? Why do people accept it? Why is it contested?' He taught us to not just follow someone else's theory blindly, and said we should question even what he taught. When students were together and someone was trying hard to argue his point, they would say, 'You are a philosopher like Professor Job! Don't bring your philosophy here!'

All the students knew which teachers took bribes because we used to talk about who we paid and how much. The teachers knew which students were rich and how big a bribe they could get from them. Professor Job was the only one who never took a bribe. He was incorruptible. Students who bribed their way through classes did not like Professor Job because this did not work with him. He taught French, which was a major subject you had to pass, and that meant there was no alternative to studying. Many students came to hate him.

Benoît was in Professor Job's philosophy class and one day he came to our home to talk to Benoît and other students. Professor Job told them that Hell and eternal punishment were lies fabricated by Catholics and Baptists to control people, and he said the students should bring arguments to contradict or oppose the teachings of the church and anyone else. The students laughed and told him, 'We don't have time to think!' When he had gone they said, 'Look at what Mr Philosophy is teaching! This is why he was expelled from the seminary. How will people stop doing bad things if there is no punishment?' But I listened, and I wanted to know why Professor Job came to those conclusions.

I finished Year 9 living in Professor Job's house. Benoît had become tired of supporting me and had started eating outside instead of buying food and bringing it home, so I had been going for two or three days without eating. When I felt hungry I drank some water to calm my stomach. When Professor Job came to our house I had asked to speak to him privately. I explained the problems I was facing and said that it was hard to survive. I said

I wanted to study and asked if he could help me to buy some food. He gave me some money to buy cassava flour to make *ugali*, the thick dough that is the staple food in Congo. He promised to speak to his wife and get back to me.

After a couple of weeks Professor Job came back and said I could live with him in his house. He could not know for sure that I was a Pygmy, but I imagine that he might have assumed it from my appearance, my morphology, although he never said anything. I was full of joy that I was going to have a meal every day. I took my things and went to Professor Job's family home, an old colonial house built by the Belgians, with running water and an indoor bathroom. He lived with his wife and his wife's younger sister, Josephine, who was studying for her teaching certificate. I stayed with them for the rest of Year 9 and all of Year 10.

School started at 7.30 am, when we had to sing to President Mobutu and his political party for 25 minutes. At 8 am we went into our classrooms and just after that the school's financial controller visited each class. He called the names of the students who had not paid their fees and they had to leave the classroom until their parents paid up. After the Mobutu stuff I would go to the toilet and return when I thought the controller had visited my class. This trick did not work for very long and I ended up being chased out of a lot of classes for non-payment.

At the end of second term, despite missing many days of school, I was ranked eighth out of 38 students. Professor Job saw that I was constantly chased from class but he was encouraged that I had come eighth so he started to pay my school fees. Really, I became a big burden on him. I was not a relative, he did not know my parents and he was also paying the school fees of his wife's sister, Josephine.

During the school holidays I mostly went back to the forest. I remember staying with my cousins Mito and Mirenge, who lived in the Kusisa forest. We had a lot of fun hunting together. There was no national park there and no restrictions so we could hunt freely. We caught lots of forest rats and *lwaki*, which are a bit like flying squirrels that jump from tree to tree. If a *lwaki* fell to the ground Mito's dog Chimbemba would catch it. If it landed on a tree, Mito or Mirenye would climb the tree to make it jump again and we would follow it through the forest. Mito and Mirenye never went to school. School meant nothing to them.

At the Bagira Institute there were teachers who asked me for bribes. I think they did not know I was poor, perhaps because I was living with Professor Job. Teachers themselves had to pay bribes to get their jobs, and then they had to recover that money by asking their students for money. One teacher said to me, 'Isaac, I know you study hard but your hand does not move.' He meant that my fingers did not move with money. I reported one teacher to Professor Job and he said, 'Don't worry about it. That is the system and we can't change it.' However, he also said that I should make sure I got the grade to which I was entitled and that the teacher did not reduce my mark because I did not pay a bribe. He encouraged me to continue studying hard instead of trying to bribe people to pass, so I concentrated, did my homework and I did pass.

This was such a happy time for me, and after a few months it got even happier. Josephine, the younger sister of Professor Job's wife, was from the Shi tribe and her family was rich. Her uncle was a judge. She was pretty and petite, with copper-coloured skin, and always had her hair done at the salon. She was a city girl and had never been in the forest or worked on a farm. I fell in love with Josephine. I had always been polite to her and whatever she told me to do, whether it was washing dishes or clothes, I would do it. 'Isaac,' she told me, 'if you continue to be polite like this, you'll be a good husband!' To my surprise, she fell in love with me and we agreed to get married. I think she thought that if she married me she could manipulate me. She had noticed I had an inferiority complex and she liked that because she thought she could control me, instead of marrying a Bantu man who would boss her around and beat her. But we kept our relationship a secret because Professor Job and his wife would never have supported it. They would have killed me if they had found out!

In fact, Josephine had two other candidates interested in her so she had a choice. I used to tell her, 'You're rich, I'm poor. How can we marry?' 'Money doesn't matter!' she would reply. 'We'll both get teaching jobs and go and live in another town.' And we planned how to leave Bukavu and make a life together.

I had the opportunity to have sex with Josephine but we were both too scared. When I had been a student in Baptist School we were taught that fornication was a sin: if you did it with someone who was not your wife you would go to Hell, where you would burn day and night. Not to die, but to suffer in eternity. At school we saw pictures of people in Hell and these terrified me.

Mama had seen that I was not showing interest in girls and asked other boys, 'Does Isaac have girlfriends?' 'No,' they told her. 'Isaac says those who have sex will go to Hell.' Mama started to think I was impotent and told everyone this. It was very embarrassing.

When I reached puberty my body transformed, and I had some friends who started to have sex with girls. But what I had learnt at the Baptist School stayed with me. I thought my friends would be punished one day and they would burn in Hell.

Then I met Professor Job and I started to question everything. I asked him to tell me the truth about Hell. He had been a priest so I knew he would know. Professor Job told me: 'No, there is no Hell where God puts bad people. Religion teaches this to stop people doing bad things.' He also explained that the consequence of having sex with someone who is not your wife is sexual disease, and not having sex before you are married is about health. He didn't know that I'd also been thinking about the consequences of sleeping with his sister-in-law. I knew that if we had been discovered I would have been chased out of the house, and Professor Job was paying my school fees. So I remained scared of having sex.

At the end of Year 10 everything changed for me. Professor Job got sick with epilepsy. He started to fall over every day and could no longer teach. I was going home for the summer holidays and planned to bring back money to repay Professor Job and to continue on to Year 11. I calculated that my chickens, which included the miracle hen, must have multiplied many times and made plans to sell them.

I got back to Bunyakiri to terrible news: there were only two adult hens left and ten chicks. I had been expecting about forty. I asked Mama what happened. 'An eagle came and ate them,' she said, 'and then a serval [a kind of wild cat] came and ate the rest.' I didn't believe her and asked my sister, Zania, who said, 'When the hens laid eggs Mum and Dad starting eating the eggs instead of letting the chickens sit on them, but in the end we just ate the chickens.'

At the end of the summer holidays when it was time for me to return to Bukavu I had only six chickens left. I sold four to pay for my bus ticket and left two with my parents because I felt I needed to give them something. As my clothes were basically my school uniform, I had worn it out and needed to buy a new one but I could not afford to buy one, or any books.

I returned to Professor Job's house with empty hands, unable to give any money to them. His wife was not happy with me. I had used their water, soap, electricity and food, then gone on two months' holiday and returned with nothing. She must have wondered if I was ungrateful or took them for granted. And her husband was sick. The whole family was unhappy. Professor Job said nothing but I could tell he was not enthusiastic towards me any more. Still, he said I could stay and finish Year 11. As I had finished Year 10 I could teach in a primary school, but if I finished Year 11 I could teach in a high school and get a higher salary.

Life became hard for them and for me. I felt I should contribute to living costs in the household but was not able to do so. I lost the strength to stay with Professor Job's family, especially as they were having a difficult time themselves. Before the end of first term I decided that I would drop out of school and return home to do something else. 'Okay, you can go,' Professor Job told me, 'but if you work for one year, save some money and then you should return to finish school.' In 1980 I left his house and went back to Bunyakiri to look for work.

Professor Job had a huge impact on me and the way I thought. It was because of him that I became so keen to question things and to use logic, not beliefs, to guide my thinking. It was also because of him that I became interested in the Jehovah's Witnesses.

In Australia I occasionally receive news of Professor Job, who has grown old and still suffers from epilepsy. Eventually I was able to send him some money, but I never did finish Year 11. I regret this but my financial situation was hard so I had to accept the situation.

When I left Bukavu I also left Josephine, who continued her studies. I had decided that I really couldn't keep my promise to her. If I married her I would give her a hard life because she could not farm or go into the forest. Months after returning to Bunyakiri I received the news that she had married one of her other candidates. Another teacher. It was probably a good thing. I wasn't ready to get married. I had no house, no money and no dowry to give her family. Josephine's husband eventually became the principal of the Congolese embassy school in Rwanda, and she had a good life there.

9

Town girls can't collect firewood

In BaTembo culture we have a saying: 'The one who is born alone dies like lice.' It means that if you live without family no-one notices if you die. But if you marry and have a big family, everyone will spread the news of your death and try to help your wife and children.

These ideas were going through my mind when I returned to Bunyakiri to look for work. I had memories of Josephine, I was nineteen and all the other young men of my age were already married or getting married. My family started to push me to marry as well. But unless I found work I would not be able to find a wife or go back to school. I spoke to a friend whose older brother was the pastor of a Baptist church. The church had two schools in the Bunyakiri district, and the older brother had appointed another brother the principal of the two schools. It was like a family business. The pastor told me that instead of me forcing life and trying to return to finish Year 11 and then Year 12, he might be able to find me a job in one of his schools as a teacher. The pastor said he had teachers who had only finished Year 8, so I felt optimistic I could get a position.

There were no immediate vacancies in either of the two schools. The principal put me on the waiting list, and eventually a job came up in another school in the village of Otobora. It was a long way from Bunyakiri, in the forest, and no-one wanted to teach there. Because of my financial situation I went, but I only lasted a month.

I got malaria and had to return to Bunyakiri to get treatment. When I was better, I was employed for a short time in a Pentecostal primary school. It was a small school in the forest close to my parents' village, but here I also had bad luck.

One day I was helping Papa make a clearing in the forest to plant some crops when I injured my foot. My right Achilles tendon was ripped off the bone. In the forest there is no doctor and I went for a month with no medicine and could not return to the school. Mama and Papa collected some herbs, crushed them and put the juice on my leg but instead of healing, the wound got infected. They went to the market in town and bought some tetracycline powder, an antibiotic. They did not know I was supposed to swallow this and instead put it on the wound, so it didn't work. After about two months the wound finally looked healed, but I could tell that inside my leg the tendon had not healed properly.

I knew I could not return to teach at the school and that I had to leave the forest. One morning I took a stick and set off to walk to Bunyakiri. It took me all day but I got there at sunset. I went to see Mr Katipula, the teacher who had given me the miracle hen, and told him everything that had happened. Mr Katipula had two houses. Normally he rented the second one but it happened to be empty and he invited me to stay there. I went to the Baptist dispensary and got treatment for my wound. It took another six months before I could walk without a stick.

It was difficult to find another teaching job, or any job. I visited the principal of one school, someone I knew from when I was a student, to ask for a job. He did not have a job for me, and told me Bantu students would not want to be taught by a Pygmy and parents would complain. The principal's comments reminded me of a song the Bantu around Bunyakiri used to sing. In English it goes something like this.

> Even if you wear nice clothes like Bantu, you won't become one, you'll stay a Pygmy.
> Even if you go to school and get a diploma, the diploma won't make you Bantu.

A friend of mine from Uganda was visiting Bunyakiri around the time I was looking for a teaching job. There are Pygmies in Uganda but there were none where he lived. My friend saw how people in Bunyakiri looked down on Pygmies and said negative things. He told me, 'There is so much discrimination against Pygmies here in Bunyakiri!' He told me I should move to his part of Uganda where no-one knows about Pygmies and I would not face discrimination, and where I could have a better life.

Another friend advised me not to go back to the forest. 'Educated people should not have to go back,' he said. But schools did not want to employ me because I was a Pygmy, and my education was no use in the forest either. This same friend told me to join the Baptist Church in order to make friends and find opportunities. I could not do that, though. I did not believe in those teachings anymore and I could not be a hypocrite. He thought I was silly to worry about it. 'I go to that church,' he said, 'and drink beer like everyone else in the congregation.' But I couldn't do it. I wanted to live a free life and do what I wanted to do freely, and not pretend that I was a faithful Baptist.

In the end I started a small business out of Mr Katipula's house. On market day, Sunday, people from surrounding villages came in to Bunyakiri to sell banana wine. Sometimes they could not sell it all and did not want to carry it back home. They asked me to store and sell it for them in return for a share of the profit. During the week I could sell the wine at an expensive price, higher than on market day because on Sundays there was lots of wine available. I was able to pay the owners the low price of market days and keep the remainder of the money. I made about $10 per week. I then did the same for those people bringing dried beans for the Sunday market. I started to buy kerosene, then school books, lollies, pens and pencils. My business became a small shop inside Mr Katipula's house. Eventually I saved enough money to set up a stall on the street in the town centre where there were lots of customers.

It was while I was running this stall that I first started to notice the Josephine who became my wife. I already knew about Josephine through her grandmother, who was a Pygmy from the Mafuo Chiefdom, like Mama's mother. Both Josephine and her mother were Pygmoid. Every day on their way to their plot outside town where they grew vegetables, Josephine and her mother would walk past me and I would look at her. I remember flirting with her like it was yesterday!

Because of Professor Job's influence I had started going to Jehovah's Witness meetings in Bunyakiri, and I used to see Josephine there as well. Only a few people attended meetings in those days because Congolese did not like Jehovah's Witnesses. Their missionaries couldn't speak French and people said it was an English church. Congolese liked the Italian Catholic missionaries. They were the first to come to Congo in the nineteenth century, and they fought with the Arabs and tried to put an end to slavery. Where I am from in Congo we say the Italian Catholic priests are the first Christian prophets in Congo – and they also preached against the Jehovah's Witnesses.

When I first met Josephine I did not have enough money to get married, but Mama and Papa were pressuring me and I had been thinking about things. I decided it was better to marry someone who could adapt to where I lived, and Josephine was from Bunyakiri. However, I faced the same problems as with the other Josephine, Professor Job's sister-in-law. First, her father was a Bantu – although *I* knew her grandma was a Pygmy – and Bantu have superiority over us. Second, her family was well off, at least compared to my family and others in Bunyakiri. Her father was a watchman for a mining company so they had a steady income and a comfortable life. I could tell her family was wealthy because her father had two houses and both had iron sheeting on the roof, and they had a battery-powered record player they used to listen to music and to dance. Third, Josephine did not know the forest at all, so another challenge was simply how to take her to meet my parents in the village where they were living. The biggest challenge, though, was that I decided I would have to find a way to live in a town because it would be hard for Josephine to live in the forest.

There were some other girls, but I felt I could not marry them as I thought they were inferior to me. They had never been to school, could not write their name and had never even seen a car before. I needed to marry someone of a higher level. So I asked Josephine to marry me. I told her, 'I am happy when I look at you. You attract me. I want to marry you and I am not joking. I love you and if you accept to marry me that would be so good.'

'I can't get married!' Josephine replied. 'I'm only sixteen! I need to be at least twenty.' I told her that other girls get married at sixteen and that it was not too young. She said that she would give me her reply another day. This was in December 1980. After that conversation I kept asking her if she had an answer for me. In January I asked again, and she told me, 'No, I'm not ready. I'll give you an answer later.'

Josephine had another young man who wanted to marry her. A Bantu. My competitor. She was having doubts about me because some family members were telling her that my family lived in the deep forest. 'How could you think of living there?' they asked her. Because she was not quite sure where I was from, she came to ask me. When I told her 'the Kasachi Forest', she had never even heard of the place! I told her that although that was where I was from, it was not where we were going to stay if we married.

There was a lady who knew me well and was friends with Josephine's mother. 'Isaac is a good boy, I know him,' she told Josephine's mum. 'If your daughter marries him, she would have found a good husband.' However, like me, my competitor had been telling Josephine that if she married *him* they would not go back to the forest and would stay in town. But my competitor was from a forest even further away than the Kasachi Forest. In the end Tuteene, Josephine's brother who I knew from primary school in Bunyakiri, convinced Josephine that I was better than my competitor and told her that as both me and my competitor were from the forest this should not influence her decision. In March 1981, three months after I first proposed, Josephine finally accepted.

We went to tell Josephine's parents of our decision. Her mother did not support us but she told Josephine, 'If that is your choice, and you love him, I can't stop you marrying.' Her parents then asked that my parents pay a dowry of 3500 makutas, about $400 at the time. In their life my parents have never earned even $100 or had any assets. I told Josephine's parents that I had 1500 makutas, which was all my money, and that I did not expect to get ten cents from my parents because they did not have it. Josephine's mother said she knew my parents did not have any money but it was the custom to ask for a dowry. She said that if I could bring the 1500 makutas they would accept that, according to the tradition. I got the money and gave it to my parents, who gave it to Josephine's parents.

Mama was not happy. 'Look,' she said, 'you are marrying someone from a rich family. Town girls don't know how to look for crabs or firewood, and she is not going to be able to walk far. She won't even be able to walk to our home!' Where my parents lived was a long way from Bunyakiri and Mama wanted me to marry a girl from the forest. Papa didn't say anything.

On 1 July 1981, a Wednesday, we went to the registry office and got married. Four days later Josephine and I set off from Bunyakiri to visit my parents. Zombanyi, Josephine's eight-year-old half-sister, came with us. She and Josephine were close, and Josephine wanted some support.

Because Josephine was meeting my parents for the first time she dressed in nice clothes: a red blouse, a white wrap-around skirt with a zebra-print pattern, and black shoes. She asked me how long it was going to take to walk there, and I lied: 'two or three hours'.

Two hours after leaving Bunyakiri we entered the forest. Zombanyi was exhausted already and could not walk any more. I put her on my back and carried her for half an hour, then she walked until she was tired again. 'How can anyone live here?' Josephine commented. She took off her shoes and carried them in her hand because they were no good on forest paths. We continued like that, with me carrying Zombanyi and Josephine becoming more and more tired. We kept walking and walking, and Josephine's heart become down. It was the first time she had ever walked a long way like that. Finally, after walking for nine hours we arrived at my parents' village.

In my parents' hut there were no chairs or tables. They had chopped tree trunks into blocks, and when she arrived Josephine had to sit on one of these in her red blouse and white wrap. She looked very different to the other women. None of them could afford to buy the kind of clothes she was wearing. Josephine was unhappy and I tried to calm her down. 'I just wanted to show you where my parents live,' I said. 'We are not going to live here ourselves.' My parents had a typical Pygmy hut made from a frame of sticks, and walls and roof made of leaves, with a low doorway. Josephine came from a house with iron sheeting on the roof and her mother had nice cooking pots, and when her family ate they each had their own plate. My family had only two pots and one metal plate with holes in it that had been patched up. When we ate together we all sat around the big metal plate and took our food from it with our hands. This made Josephine uncomfortable. She was worried she would catch something and become sick.

In Bunyakiri Josephine was friends with a young Italian novice nun who worked at the Catholic church. The church was built on land belonging to Josephine's Pygmy grandmother. The friend had taught Josephine and other young ladies the rules of hygiene and how a girl can get pregnant. All of this made Josephine think she was going to become infected with some illness during the stay at my parents' village. She was unhappy when eating and, although she did not say anything, my parents could tell there was a problem.

'Why is she so unhappy?' they kept asking. I asked Mum and Dad if Josephine and I could eat separately, from our own plate, but they did not have a spare plate! I insisted and eventually they found another plate somewhere and that is what we used for the rest of the week.

Finally, on Sunday, after a long week, we returned to Bunyakiri. I was thinking it was lucky Josephine had already signed the marriage register, because that meant she could not change her mind about our marriage.

After we got married Josephine's older sister came to stay. She was very upset that Josephine had married me. 'Even if he is educated,' she told Josephine, 'he is still a Pygmy and his parents still live in the forest. If you had waited you could have gotten a nice man, not a Pygmy.' She talked to a neighbour of mine, Moni, and criticised me – in my own friend's house! 'I don't know how my parents accepted that my sister married a Pygmy!' Moni told her that as I was already her brother-in-law she should be nicer to me. Josephine was not too bothered by her sister's comments because I had already told her that I was not going to take her back to the forest.

10

Bring our daughter back

Let me tell you how Pygmies view children. If there are many in the family, you can bring home more food. If you are a family you can easily catch an antelope and everyone has meat that day. In Pygmy culture the more boys you have, the more successful hunting will be and the more meat the family will have. I grew up knowing these things, but before I got married I was not thinking about children at all. I just wanted to leave Bunyakiri to find a better job.

In Bunyakiri we eventually found a house to live in, so we did not need to live with Josephine's family any more. It was a friend's house, a round thatched hut about 3 metres in diameter, with a small area divided off to create a bedroom. The problem was that I only had my stall. I relied on Josephine's family for living costs. If we wanted meat, fish or salt we had to get money from her family and this made me unhappy. Getting a proper job in Bunyakiri was hard. You had to be close to the American missionaries to get a job or be from the family of a Congolese pastor otherwise you had no chance. Nearly all the schools (certainly the good ones) were run by a church and to be a teacher you had to be related to someone in the church that ran that school. I was qualified to be a teacher, but I was a Pygmy and was not related to anyone important.

Although I could not find a job, I felt happy to be married. On our wedding night I had the sensations that men have, and I had sex for the first time. I had just heard about sex before: that it was good and gave pleasure. It was exciting to be able to finally do it.

I still remember the day in August, one month after we got married, when Josephine told me she had missed her period and thought she was pregnant. 'How?!' I asked her. I had learnt biology in school and knew how pregnancy happens, but I could not believe I had got someone pregnant. Because I was so new to sex I thought we were just playing and I really could not believe this 'play' had caused pregnancy.

I was happy to think I was going to become a father. Other young people my age had already had babies, so I felt I was joining their club. Becoming more of an adult. Growing up I had also heard those Pygmy sayings, like 'The one who is born alone dies like lice' and 'If you are not related by blood, do not go hunting dangerous animals together' so after the shock of getting Josephine pregnant I started to feel good about it.

After I found out Josephine was pregnant I started thinking responsibly. I went out and bought two sets of baby clothes: one in case the baby was a girl, and one in case it was a boy. In Congo when a wife gets pregnant you have to buy her a gift, a wrap she wears around her waist and legs. Not just any wrap, but Dutch wax cloth, which is very strong cloth, with beautiful patterns and bright colours. Dutch wax cloth is very popular and the price starts from $200 and goes up to $600. You can get fakes from China but there is nothing like the real thing. I bought Josephine some of this cloth. She still has the cloth I bought her when she was pregnant with our sixth child, Abishay, 22 years ago.

Another thing we do in Congolese culture is that when someone gives birth we visit to see the baby and bring them gifts, usually food and practical things, so having a baby is a very positive thing for the family. If we visited someone with a newborn baby without any gifts the parents would be very offended. They would think we did not want to welcome their child.

When Josephine was close to giving birth her family told me to take her to the maternity hospital in a nearby town, and helped me pay the costs. Josephine gave birth and we brought home our first child: a daughter we named Jamaa. Josephine's family bought us a big goat.

When Jamaa was born she looked just like me – she still does – but the first thing I did when I brought her home was to contact Mama. I remembered what Mama had told people when I was a teenager, about me being impotent. 'Now I have a baby,' I told her. 'You have been telling everyone I'm impotent, but who does this baby look like?' All Mama said was: 'That's what I've been wanting you to do.'

By this time, after about a year of running my small business – the stall on the footpath in the town centre – I managed to save enough money to buy a cheap piece of land and we built a small hut. Our own home.

Like everyone else, Josephine and I argue occasionally and when we have arguments Josephine tries to show superiority over me. Not because she is from a comfortable home, but because she is from a comfortable race. When someone has Bantu blood there is always a superiority complex over a Pygmy. Even in my own house! Or, if I make a mistake she tries to attribute it to me being a Pygmy and not something else.

When Josephine's Pygmy grandmother was a girl a Bantu man got her pregnant but he did not want to marry her. His family could not accept a Pygmy woman into their family. After giving birth to Josephine's mother, her grandmother lived with a Pygmy man, so Josephine's uncles and aunts from that marriage are all 100 per cent Pygmy. Some Pygmoids have pride and a superiority complex over Pygmies, and Pygmies can think the same way. Every young Pygmy boy does whatever he can to marry a Bantu girl, to try to reduce his own inferiority.

One of the main things Josephine and me argue about is Mama. They do not get on. The first reason they do not get on is that Mama did not want me to marry a girl from a rich family. Then when Josephine came to my parents' village for the first time she was unhappy and made it obvious to my parents. After that visit, no-one from Josephine's family visited my parents. Josephine herself never went back to their village ever again. When I bought the plot of land and built our own house in town Mama wanted me to marry another woman, someone from the forest who was the same level as her and who would kick Josephine out.

After Josephine had our first daughter, Jamaa, and was pregnant with our second child, Deborah, I stayed in town for a whole year to be near my wife. I was also trying to adapt my life to others in the town and not follow the life of the village. I did not want to go back to the forest to visit my parents, but Mama blamed Josephine. Mama also blamed Papa for me wanting to stay in town. 'I told you not to send your son to school,' she said, 'because he will want to live in town. It will change his thinking and he won't want to live in the forest.' But Papa hadn't sent me to school. He never encouraged me to go. I'm still the only one in my family who has been to school. My sisters were just trained in finding wild yams in the forest and bringing home food for the household. That's it.

I had the desire to learn and because of this I eventually left Mr François' farm to finish middle school and go to high school. And Mum was right – it did change my thinking.

But the main reason Mama and Josephine do not get on is because Mama tried everything she could with witchcraft to kill Josephine.

Mama thought Josephine was controlling me, and told me the reason I did not return to the forest was because Josephine had used witchcraft to make me change my mind and beliefs – to turn me against her and Papa. So Mama went to a witchdoctor to ask for magic herbs more powerful than those she thought Josephine had given me, to kill the power of Josephine's magic. Mum tried to get me to eat these herbs and she placed others where I was sitting or stepping. The herbs did not work. She saw that I still did not want to return to the forest.

Mama then went to a woman who was known to be a sorceress, Nagabushu. Mama asked if Nagabushu could kill Josephine so I could marry a second wife. Mama said that if Josephine were to die while pregnant with Deborah, people would think it was because of the pregnancy and would not suspect witchcraft. Nagabushu got upset and started fighting with Mum. 'I'm not a sorceress!' she shouted. 'I've never killed anyone!' She said it was Mama who was the sorceress because she wanted to kill her own daughter-in-law. Nagabushu yelled out to people, 'This woman wants to kill her daughter-in-law!' Mama had thought she would get a positive response from Nagabushu, but instead her visit created conflict with everyone. Josephine's family heard about what happened and became upset. 'Don't kill her!' they said. 'If you don't like our daughter just bring her back to us.'

11

Surrounded by crocodiles

From 1965 to 1997 Congo was ruled by President Mobutu. He put an end to all the rebellions after independence in 1960 and unified the country. Because of this he wanted all Congolese to worship him. Mobutu also wanted to rid the country of colonial legacies and make its identity more African. He changed the name of Congo to Zaire and banned people from having European names. He changed his own name from Joseph Mobutu to Mobutu Sese Seko, putting the family name first in keeping with African custom. He used to call himself 'Father of the Nation', but he did not have the qualities of a real father, like empathy or pity. If you criticised him, you were killed. That old dictator did a lot of bad things, and the support he got from the United States makes some Congolese hate America a lot.

Mobutu concentrated all power on himself and made himself into a god. He killed his opponents publicly, by hanging them in the street to make people scared. Congolese asked themselves, 'Where are our human rights?' No Western country ever spoke out against Mobutu for doing these things. They supported him. He established different agencies and a Youth League for his political party – although anyone over eighteen could join – it even had 60-year-old members. He put secret police in every corner of the country and appointed pastors and priests to positions in the Office of Judicial Police, which meant they became like magistrates. He gave them formal bureaucratic power to judge people. On top of this, Mobutu made some pastors officials of the National Order of the Leopard – an organisation he controlled directly. Pastors were happy to have this power. Mobutu morally corrupted everyone: Christians, Muslims, they all came under his control.

Mobutu developed an ideology called 'Mobutuism', which was a bit like a religious ideology with Mobutu as the highest, immortal, being. When I was in school attending religion classes, we were taught that we should only worship God, that he is the supreme being and that we should not worship other people or things. I wondered how we could worship Mobutu in the same way. Because I was against Mobutu I did not pay too much attention to Mobutuism. A lot of people working in government administration were also against the Mobutu regime but they couldn't say anything.

Mobutu tried to distract people from the suffering in their daily life with dancing. He created centres of dance in every town, and you had to do dances for Mobutu and about Mobutu. At one stage all girls were required to register for these dance centres. The Youth League would take girls there by force. If they discovered you had been hiding your daughter they would fine you or put you in gaol, and ask for money to release you.

Before any gathering (including at schools), at the opening of businesses for the day, marketplaces, and even at church we had to sing about Mobutu. A lead singer would sing out, 'Mobutu will live forever and ever,' and we were supposed to respond.

> Mobutu Oye!
> Mobutu is the most superior!
> Yes, Mobutu will live forever and ever.

If someone saw you were not moving your lips and reported you, you could get in a lot of trouble. Everyone hated this but it was dangerous to say so openly. You could speak freely in your own home but not outside – only within the close family. If you were with two or three people you trusted you might criticise Mobutu, but you did not trust people you did not know very well. If there was a conflict between people, someone might go to the Youth League and make false reports against you to get revenge. The population used Mobutu's system to settle personal grievances.

The good thing Mobutu did was that whenever the government discussed Pygmies he said that we were citizens, just like Bantu, although we were not recognised as citizens until the mid 1970s. Mobutu never took any actions to improve or change anything, such as support for Pygmies to send their children to school, so saying we were citizens was just something he announced; but at least he said it. However Bantus turned it into a joke. After Mobutu made a speech announcing that Pygmies were citizens just like everyone else and that we should be given identity cards, instead of saying, 'Bonjour Isaac' as they normally would, Bantu started to call out behind me or greet me with, 'Oh, citizen! Hello citizen!' Pygmies were very embarrassed by the whole thing.

When Mobutu first took power the economy of Congo was strong, but in the 1980s he dragged it into a big hole then buried it. People in the countryside, such as around Bunyakiri, suffered a lot. Bantu and Pygmies who lived in the forest would come to the roadside or into town to sell smoked meat or fish. Members of the Youth League would wait for them on the roads leading into town. They would ask for ID documents and when we handed them over they would ask for money to return the documents or put us in gaol unless we paid a bribe, or they would just take our goods. Of course if we didn't have any ID documents that made everything worse. If people refused to pay they were arrested and only released when they paid money. It was scary for people to come into town but there was nowhere for them to make a complaint.

My stall in the Bunyakiri town centre was making money despite these problems, but it was still difficult to get enough finance to buy the goods in the first place. I looked for something to sell that was in short supply and would therefore give me a better profit despite the bad economic times. I realised there was a lot of money to be made selling pharmaceutical products.

Pharmaceuticals were in short supply because all the government hospitals were waiting to be supplied with medicines by the government, but Mobutu's regime had no money to buy drugs. Western missionaries used to run health clinics that sold medicine but most of the missionaries started to leave Congo in the 1980s because of increasing harassment by government officials, and these clinics lacked supplies. The medicine that was available was supplied by a couple of big wholesale importers that got their products from drug companies in Europe, like Sterop in Belgium and Roche in Switzerland. There is a big demand for drugs in Congo, particularly for things like anti-malaria drugs, but they are expensive and hard to obtain, especially European products.

Selling medicines in Congo is a business with lots of hassles. There are many laws and regulations, and many penalties. If government officials find someone breaking the regulations, that person could be put in gaol for six weeks. In other areas of business no-one bothered to uphold the law, but officials really upheld pharmaceutical regulations because they knew they could make money. People selling medicinal drugs got scared because the penalties were so tough, and they paid bribes to the officials instead of arguing or risking imprisonment. Government officials insisted they had the right to arrest people because they were selling drugs illegally and under the law they did have the right to do this. But there were no other medicines! The illegal medicine sellers were saving lives by supplying drugs.

Despite all the trouble, I decided the pharmaceutical industry was a good business for me to enter. I started illegally selling medicine on the street in 1982, after Jamaa was born. I did not have a licence to sell pharmaceuticals but when I got caught by the authorities I would pay some money and continue. If you pay the officials they leave you alone; then you keep paying them; then you become friends.

By 1983 I managed to save and borrow – from Josephine's mother – enough money to buy a small piece of land in the town centre. I built a timber house and planned to open a pharmacy. I went to ask for a licence from the Regional Pharmacy Inspectorate in Bukavu, but licences were tough to get. Hospital officials did not want pharmacies around competing with them because the people working in hospitals, even in government hospitals, wanted to make a profit. Under the law there were lots of restrictions: pharmacies needed to be in a brick building, painted white on the inside, and clean and tidy, and the seller needed to be a pharmacist or qualified nurse. Under the law, a team of inspectors had to inspect the building and the qualifications of the person, but this was not followed. I tried to build a relationship with the Inspector of Pharmacies in order to get the licence but I had to give him something. If the government asks $100 for a licence, you have to give the inspector $500 – five times what the licence costs – otherwise there is no hope of getting it. I bought a licence and started selling medicine out of my building.

I always tried to get good medicines. Those from Europe were genuine and all the doctors trusted them, unlike drugs made in India, Kenya or China. For example, a tablet might be supposed to have 250 mg of an ingredient but if tested in the laboratory you will find it has only 200 mg. This means the patient might have to buy more tablets to get the right amount of the ingredient. European drugs did not have this problem.

I bought two books called *Notions des Pharmacologie* and *Aide Memoire Pour les Dispensaries*. These books were very important. I was conscious that medicine is poison if not used properly. In Congo many people cannot afford to go to a doctor so they self-diagnose and spend their money on medicine rather than a doctor. They would come to me and say they had malaria and ask what medicine to buy, and I would consult my books. There were categories of medicine for different illnesses, such as anti-diarrheal medicines or analgesics, and how to use them, and the books gave me ideas of how to prescribe drugs. Before selling to someone, I used the books to explain to the customer how to use the medicine properly. Drugs from England, Germany and the United States had instructions written in English, not in French, so I also bought a bilingual dictionary to understand how to use these medicines.

From the mid 1980s there was a lot of harassment of civilians by President Mobutu's officials: police, army, party officials, everyone. People in the countryside and the forest only came to town once or twice a year because of all the harassment they experienced from these officials for bribes and payments. Men sent their wives and daughters into town to sell bush meat or cassava because the women would be breastfeeding or have children with them so were less harassed. If men came to town they would get arrested on a pretext. There is no medicine in the countryside, so these customers came to me. They preferred my pharmacy because they trusted me. They knew I was also from the forest. If a customer had died it would have been very bad for my reputation, and I never once experienced such a case. I gave good service.

On many occasions, local administrative officials tried to close my pharmacy. They asked for $500 because I was selling out of a timber building and I was not a qualified pharmacist. I would offer $100 and they might refuse, or sometimes they would take it and insist on the remainder later. Other officials came to ask me for money as well and it became a burden. Other people in the pharmacy business were harassed in the same way.

I went to Bukavu to meet with the Regional Inspector of Pharmacies. He said, '*I* decide who opens a pharmacy and when a pharmacy should be closed, not small officials in Bunyakiri.' He said that as a pharmacy owner, I reported to him and that under the law, local officials did not have the power to close my shop. Local officials were intimidated after that and when I offered small bribes they took them and did not ask for more. It became a negotiation instead of just their demand on me. I preferred to keep a good relationship with them by paying them some money because what I was doing was illegal. The payments bought peace. It was also the only way to remain in the pharmacy business.

In Congo there has been no rule of law until now and if there is a way a Congolese can take your shirt, he'll take it. Everyone looks to convert you into cash and doing business is like being surrounded by crocodiles. You have to feed them a bit to keep them away. First of all, there is a lot of corruption, so you have to make friends with those on top. For these reasons I first built a relationship with the Inspector of Pharmacies, because he was in the domain most important to me – pharmaceuticals. Second, I built a relationship with the Chief of Police. I had to bring him something to create the relationship. Then there was a magistrate who had been introduced to me by a lawyer. I gave the magistrate $200 and he told me, 'Whenever you have a problem come to my office and I'll help if I can. I know you business people always have problems.' If someone came and tried to create a problem I showed him the magistrate's business card and that would make him go away. When making these relationships you have to make them in the right order, starting with those specialised in your business.

The other problem is that public officials go outside their positions, over their power, to intimidate people to get money. For example, if someone worked for the Department of the Environment he might come to the pharmacy and say he needed to see the diploma or qualifications of the people working there. Even the local *mwami* might come in and ask to see the licence of the pharmacist! And the Territorial Administrator, he would ask to see it as well. You have to pay them all something.

You have to pay attention to them because they are all corrupted. If you ignore them or tell them to go away, they will say you insulted them. They create a problem so they can get money from you. With some of them you can bargain. Say the Chief of Police comes and tells you he will close your shop, and then asks for $500 or $1000. According to the law, he cannot close your shop because he is a police officer and not from the Inspectorate of Pharmacies. You show your licence and say you are allowed to be open, and offer him $200 to go away. He refuses because this is too low. You then go to the Inspector of Pharmacies, who will tell the Chief of Police that he has no power to close the shop. You have already paid the Inspector of Pharmacies and that is why he will write the letter. He will just ask you for a little more money to do it. But the Chief of Police will complain that you went to someone senior – the Inspector of Pharmacies. He will say, 'You said that I did something wrong to this senior person.' And he did! But you can't have this bad relationship with the police. He will ask for the $200 he refused to take the first time and you give it to try to have a good relationship with him. Even if you have a letter from the top, from the Inspector of Pharmacies, you still have to give him something. Next time the Chief of Police comes, even if he asks for nothing you give him something, such as $20, to keep a good relationship.

Another example is a magistrate, someone who has the power to pronounce the death penalty. He might get $100 per month – but his rent could be $150 per month and then he has to pay school fees for his children. If he sits in his office all day he will never make enough salary to cover his costs, so he sends people to go and create some kind of infraction at a business, and tells them to bring the business owners to him.

That's how the system is in Congo! You have to get used to this system if you are going to survive. Corruption is the way everyone lives and they are used to it. There is no shame. If you complain to the boss of a soldier or of a police officer, the boss will take more money from you. If you complain, you will get yourself into more trouble. It is a hard system to live in. You have to know your domain. You have to know the predators and where they come from.

Despite all of these problems the pharmacy business was very profitable for me and I recruited three agents to expand it further. I would give them the medicines in advance and each week they paid me back my share of the profits. One of my agents was my old neighbour, Moni, the one who had told Josephine's sister she should stop complaining about Josephine marrying a Pygmy. I asked the police not to harass him and the other agents. The main reason I became successful was because I gave credit. Local government hospitals and clinics did not have the money to buy medicines to sell in their pharmacies, and wholesale pharmaceutical importers had many customers and did not need to give credit. So local hospitals and clinics bought from me and paid me back after one or two months.

People trusted my products but they were not always polite about me. 'We want to go to the Pygmy man, he has good medicines,' they'd say. But they also said, 'We don't know how someone from the forest has succeeded in the medicine business!'

After a couple of years, the pharmacy business was covering all our needs. I only had two children then, which made everything easier. I could afford to start following the regulations a bit more and, in 1984, I rebuilt my Bunyakiri pharmacy in brick and hired a pharmacist, Tschambu Munganga, to run the shop. I called Tschambu my pharmacist, but no-one was a real pharmacist. The only pharmacy school in Congo was in the capital, Kinshasa, 1500 kilometres away. No-one in Bunyakiri could afford to study there. In the country it was impossible to get a proper pharmacist, but Tschambu was a nurse with one or two years of training.

The I made a mistake. In 1985, Mobutu passed a decree that the slogan, 'Mobutu will remain president forever and ever!' be shouted at schools before classes, in markets before trading and in churches before praying. The crowd was supposed to respond, 'Yes! The MPR will stay forever and ever!' The MPR was Mobutu's party, the Mouvement Populaire de la Révolution. What a farce! At that time I was studying the Bible with Jehovah's Witness missionaries from the United States. Those white people told me that this is idolatry and I agreed. Mobutu was material and he would die. I had an argument with one of my neighbours about the slogan. I told him it was as if the church was worshipping Mobutu and he was taking the place of God. It was idolatry and the church should not allow it. My neighbour reported me to Mobutu's secret police, telling them, 'Isaac Bacirongo says Mobutu won't live forever.' So I got arrested for denying that Mobutu was immortal. Josephine's younger brother had supported me during my argument with the neighbour, and he got arrested as well.

The secret police don't ask questions about whether an allegation is true, they just take you away. I was put in prison and beaten with a baton 50 times on my back and legs. I'll never forget that. The next morning and every morning after that I got another 50 strokes. The guards called it 'breakfast'. 'Bacirongo!' they called, 'it's time for your breakfast.' They told me I got breakfast because I had blasphemed the President.

The Territorial Administrator of Bunyakiri asked them to let me go but the secret police had more power than him because they answered directly to the President, and they kept me there for a week. Every day Josephine brought me food, managing to get it past the guards so I received it.

After a week I was transferred from the prison in Bunyakiri to a special prison in Bukavu run by the secret police, where they locked up critics of Mobutu. At first they put me in cell number 6, which was about 50 x 50 centimetres wide. I could not sit down and when I bent my knees they touched the wall in front of me. The guards poured water on me and I had to stand there, shivering and wet. I spent two days in cell number 6 before being put in a normal cell where I stayed for another two weeks.

I can remember some of the other prisoners. There was a man who had been a captain in the Libyan army. He was Congolese, but had gone to fight as a mercenary for Muammar Gaddafi. He was returning to Congo to visit his family when the secret police arrested him. They stole all his money, of course. There was another prisoner who insisted he was the black Jesus, so the secret police arrested him as well. Mobutu wasn't going to tolerate someone else claiming he was like God. If you said to this man, 'Are you Jesus?' he would reply 'Yes! Yes! I am Jesus.' I think he was mad.

The prison guards told us, 'This country is governed by the Leopard.' That was Mobutu's nickname. 'You are going to see the Leopard face to face,' they'd threaten. Everyone was afraid of Mobutu, even those who liked him. Even the prison guards.

One day the provincial head of the secret police, Inspector Abel, visited the prison. He worked directly for the President and he had the power to arrest the Governor of South Kivu Province. This made him proud and arrogant. Inspector Abel had each prisoner brought to his office and he asked why they were there. When it was my turn the guards told him I was a Pygmy from the Kasachi forest, a BaTembo, and that I owned a pharmacy. Inspector Abel asked if it was true that I said Mobutu would not live forever.

'Yes,' I said. 'I know no human being can live forever. From the standpoint of the Bible, and scientifically, it has been proven that everyone will die.' 'The Bible also says you should be submissive to the authorities,' Inspector Abel told me. 'I know that,' I replied, 'but that doesn't mean I have to say someone will live forever.'

Inspector Abel concluded I was an irrelevant Pygmy. He said to the guards, 'If he says Mobutu won't live forever, will this influence the population? Mobutu does not care about this one. He is nothing.'

The next morning I didn't get any 'breakfast' and was taken again to Inspector Abel. He told the guards, 'I have told Kinshasa we have people in South Kivu who are against Mobutu, but this one is a Pygmy. Kinshasa says they don't want him so he doesn't need to be sent there.' I tried asking for a letter stating that I was officially free but Inspector Abel waved me away and I was released. I went home full of pain because the muscles and skin on my back, bottom and legs had started to harden and knot from the beatings. It took months of massaging and bathing with warm water by Josephine before the skin softened and I was able to sit down properly.

12

Gifts from God

Because of my pharmacy business we were financially comfortable, but I wanted to try other businesses as well. I like farming, and rented a plot of land a kilometre from my house and grew cassava and beans for sale in the market. I started farming ducks and chickens because I knew they would reproduce quickly and I could sell them for meat. In Congo, ducks and chickens don't take much work because we don't feed them like you do in Australia. They feed themselves in the streets and in the fields, and come home in the evening. All I had to do was vaccinate them against what we call *shotoka* in Swahili, which is the disease that can spread throughout all the villages, causing everyone's chickens to suddenly get sick and die. By the end of the year I had about one hundred chickens.

We were selling vegetables and getting money, selling medicines, selling chickens, and I was eating chicken every day. I was prosperous. In addition to my original plot of land I bought another two houses, making three in total. I also bought my first car, a dark blue Toyota Stout pick-up. Everybody was talking about that car. For a Bantu to buy a car was not a big deal, but for a Pygmy from the Kasachi forest, it was huge. Everyone was asking, 'How?' I was so proud of that pick-up. Josephine was also proud. We were among the richest people in our neighbourhood.

The local police chief and mayor respected me because of my pharmacy business. If we went to a bar, it was me who would buy them beer. They would say, 'Mr Bacirongo, How are you? We are thirsty.' And I would tell them to start a tab at the bar. Behind my back people dismissed me. Some said, 'Ohhh, Bacirongo! The Pygmy,' like I was a joke. Other times when I walked down the street, people would call out, 'You might be rich, but you're still a Pygmy!' They wondered how I managed to eat and drink with the mayor and police chief. Business was good, but I was limited in what I could do in Bunyakiri.

There were also problems between Mama and Josephine, and between me and my parents.

I was the eldest son and Mama wanted a grandson. Africans, even white people, value boys more than girls but this is a mistake. When Josephine gave birth to our third child, Zawadi, Mama was not happy because we now had three daughters. Girls. Mama blamed Josephine and said, 'She's giving birth to herself!' Pygmies think that daughters continue the line of the family they marry into, so Mama wanted me to have a son to continue our family's line. But for me it did not matter and I was happy to have baby girls, and the whole thing irritated Josephine. This is why Josephine decided to call our third daughter 'Zawadi', which means 'gift' in Swahili. Because Mama had been talking so much about daughters, Josephine wanted to make the point that a third child who was a daughter was still a gift from God. When our fourth child, a son, Wetekay, was born a couple of years later, Mama was very happy.

I argued with Mama about witchcraft and the traditions she followed. In traditional Bantu culture in my area, when a king dies someone must cut off his head and take it for safekeeping to a sacred place in the forest. Bantus have assigned Pygmies responsibilities in this ceremony and it is a Pygmy man who does this. He is called a *muhombe* and is like a priest, but he must be from a Pygmy lineage. The *muhombe* has powerful magic. He wears a mask, a leopard skin across his chest, a raffia skirt and a necklace made of wild banana seeds and the teeth of wild boar. He carries his tools in a raffia bag – a few teeth of dead chiefs, and other things to help him communicate with the dead and tell the future. The special place the *muhombe* protects is called the *buhombe*. It is very sacred to Pygmies and Bantu, but Bantu are not allowed to go there. The entire head is placed on a tabernacle in the forest and the *muhombe* would watch it carefully to see if there are any movements of the skull. The *muhombe* received training in how to interpret each movement, such as to the left or to the right, because any shifting of the head signifies something. The *muhombe* cares for the site for thirty or forty years, when the role of guardian or caretaker passes to his son.

The colonial government banned the practice of cutting off the heads of chiefs in the 1920s or 1930s. After the ban, Pygmies, with the agreement of Bantu, secretly extracted teeth from the heads of dead chiefs as symbols of the head, and took these to the sacred site instead. Pygmies hid the teeth because if the colonial authorities found that the teeth had been taken from a body they would put the person in prison.

The *muhombe* in the Mafuo Chiefdom traditionally come from my family, and when I was young my father held this role. Bantus said I would have to do this when my father died as I was part of the lineage. I *refused* – for me, for all my offspring, and for all my descendants! I don't believe in these practices. The Bantu then said that as I refused to do it, my sister, Zania, the next in line in my family, would have to carry the *muhombe* assignment when Papa died. Women cannot be the *muhombe* themselves, but any sons Zania might give birth to would become the *muhombe*. 'Carrying the assignment' meant carrying the next *muhombe* in her womb. Zania was not supposed to get married because she had to dedicate herself to this assignment, a bit like a nun, but it was all right for her to give birth to the next *muhombe*.

Zania eventually became pregnant, but I knew that a first pregnancy is always problematic. A girl should go to a prenatal consultancy at least once a month when she is pregnant for the first time. And Zania was about 135 centimetres tall – that's short, even for a Pygmy. Because I had many friends at that time who were nurses, I knew that short women often have trouble giving birth because their pelvis is small. I told Mama to take Zania for a prenatal check-up, but instead she took her to the witchdoctor, who told them, 'Yes, Zania will have a child who will help the Mafuo Chiefdom.' I told Mama that the witchdoctor was lying and that Zania should go to a medical doctor. Mama refused. We have an adage, in both KiTembo and Swahili, and Mama repeated it to me. 'If you want to be misled, just follow those people who are educated because they think they know everything!' Mama was saying this about both me and the medical doctors.

When Zania was nine months pregnant Mama went back to the witchdoctor, who told her not to go to the maternity hospital. 'She will give birth,' he assured her. Eventually Zania went into labour. She was at the Pygmy village in the Kasachi Forest where Mum and Dad were living. She could not give birth, and someone came to get me from Bunyakiri. I came with some others and we made a stretcher and carried her out of the forest to a clinic run by an American. Zania didn't make much noise during the journey and was still breathing when we arrived at the clinic, but she died shortly afterwards. The clinic said that the baby should be removed and buried in its own grave next to its mum. They opened up Zania and found two little babies inside. After this one of my cousins, Maliyababa Kashishi, became the *muhombe*.

I kept thinking about my parents. About why they were poor and not able to have even two chickens when I had 100, and I wondered why they kept living this kind of life. I had bought some land for them in Bunyakiri – at that time land was not very expensive. I told my parents to move into town, and they built a house and I bought 26 pieces of corrugated iron so they could replace the thatch with an iron-sheeting roof. But Mum and Dad wanted to return to the forest. There was no meat in Bunyakiri. It was too far from the forest for hunting and there was nowhere to put snares around town. They always wanted meat. Whenever they went to the market they told the butcher to give them a couple of kilograms of meat, and as they had no money they would give him an iron sheet. 'Don't tell Isaac,' they'd tell the butcher.

Before this happened, I had visited Bukavu and bought a suit for Papa. I later saw someone else in Bunyakiri wearing that suit. I knew it was the suit I had bought Papa and that he could not have bought it in Bunyakiri. I asked the man where he got it and he told me he had exchanged it with my dad for banana wine. I had bought Papa other shirts and pants and he had also exchanged these for alcohol.

One day I visited my parents' house and found only three of the 26 iron sheets still there. They had exchanged the rest for meat. Eventually they sold all the iron sheeting, and the land, and the house I had bought them, and fled back to the forest.

This created a big conflict between me and my parents. I realised we did not understand each other. I was already thinking about leaving Bunyakiri because of my business ambitions, so when this happened I decided to leave and move to Bukavu. The family followed the following year, in 1986.

13

Any news from Bukavu?

In Bukavu I opened a second pharmacy and then a third in a small town, Minova, about 150 kilometres north of Bukavu. The business name of all three pharmacies was Djumaphar. It made me feel a bit proud to see those shops with the name painted on the front.

Business in Bukavu was not easy. It was hard to sell and there were fewer buyers for each business, and lower profits because there was so much competition. Life was still good, but business was hard. Every Monday I got about $150 from my agents and $450 from the pharmacies, for a net profit of about $350 per week or $18,000 per year. This was *a lot* of money for Congo. Most people made about one dollar a day, and I was making fifty. But people are never satisfied with what they have!

By 1991, five years after the family had moved to Bukavu, we had six children: Jamaa, who was nine; Deborah, seven; Zawadi, five; Wetekay, four; Abner, one; and Abishay, the baby. I was younger than my neighbours and they said, 'This BaTembo from Bunyakiri, he is blessed! He has three daughters and three sons. God loves you!' Josephine and I felt this as well. We felt that God loved us and that we *were* blessed.

Having so many children was not a burden for me. Even if I had nothing to give to them, I never thought it was a problem. If you don't think you have a problem, then you don't have one. We never worried and said, 'We have food for only three kids, how will we share it amongst six?' We never thought, 'What will they eat or wear, and how will we get the school fees?' In Africa, people say the one who gives us those children – God – will be the one who provides for them. But, myself, I knew I had to work hard to provide for my children. If one day I got a kilogram of flour and a kilogram of meat, we divided it and everyone had a portion, then we drank a cup of water and went to bed. The next day we would look for something else. Having more kids was not a problem and I only thought positively. I knew the solutions for how to provide for them would come.

Our house had a big living area and three bedrooms off it. One for Josephine and me, one for the boys and one for the girls. Out the back I built a separate building that housed the kitchen and another bedroom. When we had visitors they stayed there. We had a lot of visitors. Lots of Pygmies who were visiting Bukavu knocked on our door and asked for a bed for the night. There was another Pygmy family that lived in Bukavu, but no-one ever knocked on their door: that family did not welcome being associated with Pygmies and did not want to help them.

When they were young and growing I really wanted a good future for my kids. In Africa that means getting a good education, but I discovered that my kids did not all have the same abilities. I focused on investing in the most intelligent ones, who were passing without any problems and doing well. I found that putting pressure to do well on the kids who were not very good in school did not make any difference to their performance. I decided to leave these ones in a public school. This has created problems for me now. When we cannot pay our mortgage and we ask the kids for help, sometimes they say, 'Dad, you were unfair. You sent us to public school, but Wetekay to a private school. Why don't you ask him for help?' They always remind me of where I sent them to school.

With my first daughter, Jamaa, I bribed the principal of the best Catholic primary school in Bukavu to let her attend. Only a few parents could send their children there. It was not so expensive; the problem was there were not enough places. When the principal refused to enrol their children, parents would offer him money. I went five times to the principal's house and each time I found other parents there, also waiting to see him. African culture is not like Australian culture. In Australia, if someone you don't know turns up at your house and you don't want to speak to him you can talk to him through the door or tell him to go away. This is too rude for Congolese. We can't do that. We have to let people in. This means that the principal had to let all of us parents into his salon, and this gave us the opportunity to push him to accept our kids. He did not ask for money, but when I showed the cash to him he was weak. I paid him $30, which was about two weeks' salary for him. If you multiply that by the number of parents, it means the principal was making a lot from bribes. I enrolled Zawadi and Wetekay in a bilingual English–French primary school. Fees were $20 per month for each one, and this was a lot of money for Congo.

The kids helped us do chores around the house, such as washing the dishes or taking dried cassava to the mill. We used to buy lumps of dried cassava but it had to be milled so we could mix the flour with water to make *ugali* dough. Going to the mill was one of the tasks a child could do.

From the age of about thirteen, they also started wanting freedom to do whatever they wanted. The older children also wanted to control the smaller ones, to discipline them as though they were the parent, and they thought they had the right to smack them. As a parent you have to defend the smaller ones because they are powerless in front of the older brothers and sisters. If we gave an older child a task to do at home, they wanted to make their younger brothers or sisters do it.

In Africa if children do something wrong they usually get smacked or beaten by their parents. This is how most African parents discipline their children and it is a big shock for them when they come to countries like Australia and the government tells them it is illegal. Personally, if my children misbehaved I used to make them kneel down facing a wall and raise their arms against the wall while the others were out playing. That made them understand they were being punished.

Parenting in the forest was different to parenting in urban areas. In the forest you follow all the rituals and customs, but in urban areas, it is a multicultural environment with lots of different tribes. Pygmies in town, including me, didn't parent like in the forest – we copied what everyone else did around us. I had been exposed to Western culture and white people, like Miss Foss my English teacher, and I knew lots of Bantu people. For example, I didn't think I should keep my daughters from attending school, like my father did.

Ever since our first child was born, Josephine and I have shared parenting. Because we had another child every one or two years Josephine was not able to look after all the kids herself, so while she was breastfeeding the newborn I would feed the infant on the bottle. During the day I was usually out finding work and earning money and Josephine stayed home looking after the children. But when I came home I did my share. I think I got this involvement in parenting from Mama. The bad side of Mama was her infidelity, which did not make us respect her, but she was a very capable mother.

The other bad side of Mama was that she kept hiring witchdoctors to kill Josephine. In 1991, ten years after we married, Mama went to a different witchdoctor, one who lived not too far from their village in the forest. He was an older man in his forties. Mama told him that she and Papa did not get anything financially from me because I lived in Bukavu and was controlled by my wife. The witchdoctor told Mama how powerful he was. 'It will be very simple to kill your daughter-in-law,' he said. 'I have the power to bring storms, such as lightning storms. Lightning has the power to cut a palm oil tree in half. Someone died a few months ago from a lightning strike, and it was me who did that.' The witchdoctor said he knew that Mama did not have any money, but … 'If you give me your youngest daughter, Sibazuri, to be my wife that would be enough payment. If you do this, I will kill Josephine and in two weeks' time you will go to the funeral of your daughter-in-law. But because you want me to kill a person, you have to give me a person.' 'I'll give you whatever you want,' Mama told him. 'The most important thing is that our son gets rid of his wife.'

Mama told Sibaruzi that if she refused to be the witchdoctor's wife, everyone in our family would be killed. Sibaruzi did not want to go, but they forced her. Mama escorted her to the witchdoctor and when they arrived he showed them teeth of wild animals, herbs and bottles of liquids. Sibaruzi was afraid. She thought that if she refused her whole family would be killed, so she stayed and became the witchdoctor's second wife. She was twelve at the time and had not even had her first period. I still do not know how Mama could do this. What a bad heart! I told Mama once that what she did to Sibaruzi was like what happened to her, when her family forced her to marry Papa. She screamed at me. Mama feels bad about it and did not want me to remind her.

For two weeks Mum and Dad waited, preparing to go to Bukavu for Josephine's funeral. Mama kept asking everyone, 'Any news from Bukavu?' But they received no news of a death. After a couple of weeks they went back to the witchdoctor and said that their daughter-in-law had not even gotten sick. He told them: 'It is your fault because you did not tell me before that your son and daughter-in-law live in a house with electricity. When I send my force, the electricity sends it back to me. I've been trying to send my force but it comes back! You should have told me this. Now you have to be patient and wait until the electricity is cut or until they move to a house with no electricity, then my force can work perfectly.'

The witchdoctor had never been in a city. He thought electricity was like lightning but had never seen it himself. My parents believed him and told themselves that because electricity is made by white people, the witchdoctor's force would not work while the electricity was still on in my house.

They returned to their village dispirited. They waited another six months and still nothing happened. The witchdoctor then told them to wait until Josephine and I visited Bunyakiri and then it would happen – Josephine would be struck down by his force. He told them to come and tell him when we were in Bunyakiri, and then they would see that Josephine would never return to Bukavu. I knew the witchdoctor was just trying to keep Sibaruzi. When the witchdoctor failed, I also knew that he would say it was Mama's fault because of something *she* had not done. Witchdoctors are charlatans.

Mama and Papa waited and waited. After about two years, Sibaruzi discovered that her husband had been lying all along and that she had been given to him as payment to kill Josephine. Sibaruzi grew strong against the witchdoctor. Her fear of him was no longer there. She had stayed because of fear but now she stopped obeying him and returned to my parents. They told her not to go back. They realised that the witchdoctor had lied to them, or at least his magic was not very strong. He came once to ask if Sibaruzi would come back but she refused and told him she never wanted to see him again. Mama told him, 'Your power only works in your local area. It cannot reach Bukavu!'

As for how I know about Mama and the witchdoctor, that is another story.

My brother, Bahavu, stole salt and soap from the house of my sister, Machozi. Salt is very expensive in the forest, so stealing it is a big deal. Machozi went to Mama and complained, and Mama started to defend Bahavu, her son, and insulted Machozi. Machozi got upset and they started arguing. Then they started fighting physically, tearing clothes off each other.

Two months after their argument Machozi's young baby died. Machozi is a Christian so did not want to go to a witchdoctor. Instead, she went to a Pentecostal pastor and asked him to find out who killed her baby. The pastor prayed to the Holy Spirit who told her, 'Your Mama did it.' Witches communicate with demons. So if demons tell them to do something – for example, if they say 'Give me your grandchild' – the witch will do it … And everyone said that Mama was a witch.

Machozi took her dead baby to Mama and left it with her, accusing her of being a witch. Mama buried the baby, and she and Machozi became enemies. But I know that Machozi's baby died from sickle-cell anaemia and not witchcraft. My family are carriers of sickle-cell anaemia, and children with this disease often die young. Most of Machozi's children died at around two or three years old: she had twelve children and seven died. Machozi said that her children died because of witchcraft, but I assume Machozi has sickle-cell anaemia and that is why the baby died.

When Machozi became enemies with Mama, she became friends with Josephine and me. Previously, Machozi had not been so close to us. She knew about Mama hiring a witchdoctor to kill Josephine but had hid it from me. Now that we became close, Machozi told me everything. She had been with Mama when the witchdoctor explained what he would do and when he asked for Sibaruzi as payment.

14

The Tembo shop

In the early 1990s there was international pressure on President Mobutu for multi-party politics. The United States had decided it liked democracy in other countries, but up until then the only legal political party in Congo was Mobutu's. This was the beginning of the end for Mobutu's regime. In 1992 he organised a big conference in the capital, Kinshasa, and all his opponents were invited. I think he thought he could control them, but the opposite happened. Everyone started to speak out against Mobutu. When ordinary people saw this they started to speak up as well. We knew then that his power was weakening.

Unfortunately, although Mobutu was starting to weaken politically, he was still strong militarily. He gave his soldiers the power to do to civilians whatever they wanted, and they did. At that time, if a soldier saw you had a nice shirt he would tell you to give it to him. If you had a nice watch, the soldier would just take it. There was no-one to complain to about this. No official had any power over a soldier. Many times they took my own watch or shoes. 'I like your shirt. Take it off with a calm spirit. Do you want to argue with me?' they would say. Then they would ask, 'Did I rob you?' and you would say, 'No. No. You didn't rob me.' 'So go away calmly,' they'd say and you'd walk off shirtless. But before taking your shirt they would check if you had anything else worth taking. They would ask you to count out your money. If you had $50 they would say, 'With a calm spirit, give me that $50.' Then they would ask, 'Did I rob you?' and you had to say no. People ended up wearing old clothes that no-one would want to steal.

I don't know if Mobutu was actually unable to pay his soldiers and government officials, but none of them were paid. Mobutu made one speech where he told the army, police and the civil guard, 'You're asking me for salaries when you have weapons in your hands. Don't kill, but use those to get money.' They started to live off the population, to get money and to eat. Some soldiers were not happy about this, but they had to survive, so they went to the market and threatened to arrest people unless they were given money. All the government departments started to ask for money for any small service. To get a job you had to pay money, and if you were a parent with children in school you had to give something to the teachers (who were not paid at all) if you wanted your children to pass.

Even though we were being harassed by soldiers, people started to challenge everything about Mobutu's rule. They weren't happy that their Christian, European names had been banned and started using them again. I had never actually had a European name, but they sounded modern and I felt like I should. 'Isaac' sounded good to me and I wanted a short name. So my name became Lwamungu Isaac Bacirongo.

After Mobutu's power began to weaken, it seemed the regime would change and the economy would open up. I thought that if conditions improved in Congo, business might not be so good as there would be more competition in the pharmacy sector and profits would decrease. Public servants would have better conditions and higher pay, like in Rwanda where government employees were well paid. I thought I had better get a professional qualification that would allow me to join the public service if the regime changed.

For a little over a year I held a position as the administrator for a local business association, the League for the Expansion of Small Business, but as the pay was so low I kept my pharmacy business as well. However, the president of the association misspent all the money and the Scandinavian aid organisation funding it eventually stopped providing funds, so I left. I decided to go back to school to get a nursing degree and enrolled in the Institut Médicale de Bukavu. I thought that with my pharmacies and a nursing diploma, I could open a private medical clinic and work there myself. I could always get a job in the Department of Health if business conditions became bad.

Running my pharmacies and studying at the same time was difficult. A friend, Aloise, told me that even after I qualified I would not earn more than about $100 a month as a nurse. Aloise advised me to quit nursing and stick to the pharmacy business. He suggested I expand my business by importing my own pharmaceuticals, bypassing the wholesalers, through Kigali, the capital of Rwanda. Kigali is about a six-hour drive from Bukavu. Aloise knew various businessmen in Kigali and offered to introduce me to someone from a big pharmaceutical company. The idea was to buy medicines from this man, import them into Congo and then sell them in my pharmacies. It sounded like a good plan, so we went to Kigali and I was introduced to Lucien.

Lucien was Hutu who had married a Tutsi woman from a rich family. Lucien's father-in-law owned a chain of petrol stations and was one of the wealthiest men in Rwanda. Lucien himself sold pharmaceuticals. There was a lot of theft from government and NGO health clinics in Rwanda, and Lucien received the stolen pharmaceuticals and sold them on the black market. I used to buy some of them from him.

On that first trip I bought a consignment of drugs and took them back to Bukavu, and made a good profit of about $300. These visits became routine and eventually I was making two or three trips a month to Kigali, always buying from Lucien and then bringing the drugs back to Bukavu. Lucien started giving me pharmaceutical products on credit and I would pay him back later, once I had earnt money from selling the drugs in Congo. On a business trip to Uganda I also made a good relationship with an Indian man who owned a pharmaceutical factory in Kampala. I bought medicines from him as well, and imported them into Congo.

Doctors and nurses admired my pharmacy because they knew I sold good medicines and that I was going outside Congo to find them. I had a passport, spoke French and some English, and I could read and write. All of this allowed me to supply the area with pharmaceuticals. There was nobody else who could do this as cheaply.

I made a lot of money. I invested some of the profits into three vehicles, a Toyota Hi-Ace minivan, a Nissan Urvan and a Toyota Dyna truck. I hired two drivers who drove the minivans around Bukavu picking up passengers, and I employed a driver for the truck, which carried goods long distances throughout Eastern Congo. I made another $50 a day from each of these vehicles.

I became good friends with Lucien and eventually he told me not to spend my money on a hotel in Kigali but instead to stay at his home. I had my own room in his house and got to know his family and his wife very well, but I didn't tell Lucien I was a Pygmy.

Pygmies are just not going to do that if somebody already thinks we are Bantu.

One evening we were talking about racism in Rwanda. Lucien was telling me how Hutus are treated, how Tutsis are treated and how Twa, the Pygmies of Rwanda, are treated. He told me how his wife was a Tutsi from a rich family. 'Isaac,' he said, 'if someone is poor they shouldn't marry into a poor family because it will become a burden on them. They should marry into a rich family because the family will help the person get ahead. That's how I got the money to get started in my pharmaceutical business, through my wife's family.' Lucien's story about marrying into a rich family made me think about myself, and how I married into Josephine's family and had gotten a loan from Josephine's mother which had helped me start my own business. Then, when he mentioned the Twa, I felt I had to tell him I was a Pygmy because I worried he would hear about it when meeting other Congolese. I said, 'Don't be surprised if, when you go to Bukavu, people call my shop "the Pygmy shop" or "the Tembo shop" because instead of calling me by my name, people in Bukavu call me by my race.' It took him a few seconds to understand what I was saying, and I could tell he was surprised. I explained how Pygmies are discriminated against in Congo and he said, 'In Rwanda Twa are treated the same way. People say they are dirty.'

I was scared that when Lucien found out I was a Pygmy he would change his attitude towards me – that he might worry about eating and drinking with me. During our conversation I could see that his attitude towards me did change a little, but he didn't look down on me. His reaction was more like someone discovering something new. He told me, 'We are all the same before God' and I suppose this was his way of saying he did not mind. The thing is, Lucien cared about what I was doing for him – selling his medicines – and not that I was a Pygmy. He cared more about money than race.

15

Worse than Hell's fire

Even while I was doing good business in Rwanda, there was a war going on. The background to this war is a bit complicated.

When Rwanda became independent from Belgium in 1960, a lot of Tutsis fled. During colonial times Tutsis, who were a minority, had been treated better than Hutus, but when Rwanda got independence, power went to the majority Hutus – who wanted revenge against the Tutsis. The Tutsis fled to neighbouring countries – to Uganda, Tanzania and Congo – where they became refugees. These Tutsis and their children wanted to return and take power, or at least share power with Hutus. The Rwandan President from 1973 to 1994, President Habyarimana, was a Hutu and he did not want the Tutsis to come back. He already had other people – including other Hutus – who opposed him. In the early 1990s, the Tutsis decided to go back to Rwanda by force and created an army with support from Uganda. This expatriate Tutsi army started invading Rwanda from the north, from Uganda, and fought President Habyarimana's regime.

The Rwandan genocide started in April 1994 when the plane carrying President Habyarimana and the President of Burundi was shot down as it approached Kigali airport. Hutus in Rwanda were angry that their president had been killed and they blamed Tutsis. They said Tutsis had come from outside the country to kill their president and to take their land and belongings. Local militias called Interahamwe were created, and they saw any supporters of the Tutsi army as the enemy and started killing them. Hutus who opposed the Habyarimana regime, but who did not necessarily support the Tutsi army, were also killed. I had a friend in Kigali who was killed with his whole family. He was a Jehovah's Witness and a Tutsi. More than 800,000 people – Tutsis and some Hutus – died in 100 days.

When the plane carrying President Habyarimana was shot down, this affected me as well. I had been on my first business trip to Nairobi with Lucien. We had bought a big consignment of medicines and had sent it by cargo plane to Kigali. Lucien had $20,000 worth of medicines waiting at customs at Kigali airport for pick-up, and I had $5000 worth. All our pharmaceuticals were lost when the President's plane was shot down because the entire airport was taken over by Interahamwe.

Towards the end of the genocide, when Tutsi forces advancing from Uganda took control of Rwanda, millions of Hutu civilians, government officials, soldiers and Interahamwe fled into Congo. I did not see many Tutsis come into Bukavu. I suppose they were killed before they could cross.

The Rwandans who fled into Bukavu did not initially create additional insecurity for Congolese. The Rwandan population had discipline because their whole government and army had come with them, and the UN and NGOs were feeding everyone in refugee camps. Every Congolese mistreated those Hutu refugees, even poor Congolese treated them badly. Congolese used to tell them, 'You are a killer! You killed Tutsis in your country!' The Congolese were xenophobic. They don't like foreigners and they did not like those Rwandans. They just wanted to make money from them. Soldiers and police took their cars – Rwandans had nice cars compared to ours. The Rwandans said, 'These are Rwandan Government cars!' but the Congolese took everything anyway.

It was a bad time to be a Tutsi in Bukavu. The Congolese started thinking the same as many Rwandan Hutus: that Tutsis were bad people and needed to be killed because after taking power in Rwanda, we thought they were coming to take power in Congo. Any Tutsis who were found were killed by Congolese or by Rwandan Hutus. I remember travelling on the Lake Kivu ferry from Bukavu to Goma, and people calling out and pointing at bodies floating in the water. These were the dead bodies of Tutsis that had been washed down the rivers from Rwanda.

Bukavu became full of people. There were huge shanty towns and camps where refugees lived, with no roads going into these areas. We saw people suffer. Many Rwandan Hutus became beggars, but they were begging from a population that was already poor. The Hutu refugees needed to survive so they worked for very low wages, perhaps for fifty cents a day, so labour became very cheap in Bukavu. Some Congolese benefitted from this, me included. I built a house using Rwandan masons and it was cheap because the labour cost nothing. I also bought a Suzuki car and then a Mitsubishi Pajero very cheaply from Hutu refugees, about $3000 each. They were selling their cars at low prices because they knew the Congolese authorities would steal it for nothing. They figured it was better to sell it cheaply before it was stolen.

I became friends with a Hutu doctor, Dr George, who fled to Bukavu after the genocide. He helped Josephine in 1995 when she found a lump in her left breast. Josephine's mother died from breast cancer so when Josephine found the lump she was convinced it was her time to die. I was worried, although I think Josephine was suffering more from fear of dying than from pain from the lump itself. I took Josephine to Dr George and he opened up her breast and cut out the lump. Luckily it was just a lump, not cancer. And it was not a miracle: it was scientific diagnosis and treatment.

Another Hutu who fled was Lucien, who was caught up in the retreat of the Hutu forces as the Tutsi army advanced. Because Lucien's wife was a Tutsi, and because his wife's father gave money to support the Tutsis who were fighting the Rwandan government, Lucien was a target. His wife had already fled to Goma, and Lucien fled to Bukavu. To my house. He came at dusk, around 6 pm. When I opened the door, I was very surprised to see him. He looked scared. Lucien knew a lot of rich people in Bukavu but he did not go to them. In such a critical period he came to my house. It showed that he had confidence in me. He thought the only place he could be safe in Bukavu was with me. He asked to come in and told me not to tell anyone that he was in Bukavu.

The relationship and the connections between Lucien and me were deep. I had had my own bedroom in his house and I was going to Kigali at least twice a month. When he fled to me in Bukavu, I felt I had an obligation to save his life. You know those songs about Pygmies … 'Even if you are well-dressed, you can't become a Bantu; even if you have a diploma, you can't become a Bantu.' And what does 'Bantu' mean? It means 'human being'. When there is a Bantu who shows genuine friendship to a Pygmy, we become attached to them. Like Professor Job, who guided me and paid for my school fees – I still send him money. I think Lucien knew that I had a genuine strength of friendship for him that was not mixed up in hypocrisy, unlike his Bantu friends who were really just interested in doing business with him.

I took a big risk sheltering Lucien. There were a lot of Hutus in Bukavu and a lot of tension, and people were being murdered. He was well known in both Rwanda and Bukavu, and he was worried he would be killed if he was seen by Hutus from Rwanda. Josephine and I were very afraid but we hid him for three days. We locked him in our bedroom and did not let him out in case someone saw him. We told the children to close their mouths and not to say anything. We were worried that hiding someone would get us into trouble with Congolese authorities or soldiers – they would want to know why we were doing this. I was worried about Congolese threatening me and asking for money, but Lucien was scared that if Congolese found out they would tell Hutus. We did not sleep for the three days we hid Lucien.

Lucien eventually decided that he had to leave our house because by that stage there were so many Hutus from the Rwandan government living in Bukavu. That night, at around 2 am, Lucien and I left the house trying to be very quiet and not wake anyone. There were no longer any street lights in Bukavu, so it was dark. We walked cautiously, trembling with fear. On the way we saw a few other people, but they were scared of us because Lucien is tall and big. Unless you have a gun you are scared of him, especially at night. When we saw that we were safe, we hurried down to the lake shore.

Something I still don't understand is that at the lake shore there was a boat waiting to take Lucien back to Rwanda. He had somehow arranged for it to meet him, and I still don't know how because he had been locked in my bedroom and we had no mobile phones then. I saw that the people in the boats were Tutsis. Everyone was being very quiet. Lucien turned to me and said, 'Go home.' His voice sounded confident and it showed me he was safe, so I was happy to leave. The motor started and the boat went off, across the lake back into Rwanda, which was by now fully controlled by the Tutsi army. I got home about 5 am and told Josephine that Lucien had left safely.

I have lost touch with Lucien now, but in 1997 I went to see him in Kigali. He became very rich after the genocide. He was favoured by the new Tutsi government and expanded all his businesses across Rwanda. Africans are very different to Europeans. When Africans have money they usually put a big distance between themselves and poor people, so you cannot approach the rich. But Lucien let me see him and he gave me $300.

During this whole period Congolese military and police personnel would detain you or your car and ask for a bribe for you or the vehicle to be released. To survive, if you had a car, you had to pay $100 to each of the high commanders in government, military and police organisations – and there were many – if you could afford it. This way if you were caught, the high commander would intervene and get back your car for you. One day around 6.30 am Josephine and I were taking some house guests to catch the ferry on Lake Kivu, from Bukavu to Goma. On the way to the ferry port there were four or five roadblocks, each created by a different government service. To get past each you had to pay a fee, but the fees were all illegal. On our way home some soldiers with guns got into our car. They took Josephine into the back with some of them – I was driving. They told me to take Josephine home and then said I had to drive them around. I didn't have the chance to find one of their commanders. I drove them around, all over town, like a taxi driver until about 2 pm when my petrol finally ran out and they got out and let me go.

We suffered a lot in the 1990s because of this kind of behaviour from soldiers and because everything became corrupted. The whole population was depressed, and we didn't cope. The one thing we had was our families. Even then, when there was no security or certainty, nobody thought about family planning because our big families helped us with life. Mentally, we wanted Mobutu's regime to end but we did not know how to end it. We felt we were destined to suffer. A friend of mine, Déo, used to say, 'We will not suffer in Hell because the life we live in Congo is worse than Hell's fire and we are already used to it. The people who will suffer are the Europeans, because they aren't used to suffering!'

16

Speaking with one voice

In the mid 1990s, while Mobutu was still clinging to power and when Bukavu was full of Rwandans, a man in Bukavu called Kapupu created a small non-profit organisation to help Pygmies. Kapupu publicly called himself King of the Pygmies, but he was not a Pygmy at all; he was from the Rega tribe. He asked members of his church, the Bahá'i church, to donate salt and second-hand clothing that he could distribute to Pygmies. The Pygmies were very upset about this, that this man was saying he was their king. Traditionally we don't even have chiefs – let alone kings! Kapupu said other things like, 'All the Pygmies are naked so I'm giving them clothes.' He would tell Pygmies, 'I am going to take you away from nakedness.'

One day I was invited to visit the office of a man called Kabungulu who worked for Héritiers de la Justice, a local human rights organisation. Kabungulu was a handsome man in his late forties. He was slim, and didn't have a big tummy like me. He laughed and joked a lot and had a kind manner. He was a Bantu, and a Rega like Kapupu and from the same area as him. Kabungulu had heard what Kapupu had been saying and told me, 'If Kapupu is saying he is your king, it is the fault of the Pygmies because you are hiding. You do not come out and take the lead in saying he is an imposter. You have to raise your voice, you need to do something about it. I cannot approach the wealthier Pygmies living in Bukavu because they don't want to be known as Pygmies. But I can talk to you.'

Kabungulu knew there were Pygmies who were capable of being leaders and fighting for Pygmy rights but that shame was keeping them back. 'There is an organisation in London,' he said, 'the Forest Peoples Programme. It wants to bring all the Pygmies together so they can speak with one voice and be proud. To help you.' Kabungulu told me to contact people in my community so we would all come together.

I was reluctant to get involved. When Kabungulu first contacted me I wondered what I was going to gain. It was dangerous to be an activist in Congo and I thought about the time I had been arrested for denying that Mobutu was immortal. Mobutu used to hang his critics in public, so setting up a human rights organisation during his reign was impossible. An environmental or business organisation might be possible, but not something for human rights. Héritiers de la Justice itself had only been established in the early 1990s when Mobutu's power had started to weaken.

Like other Pygmies, I had also hidden my identity and told people I was BaTembo in an effort to pass as Bantu, although being BaTembo still meant I was nothing. The reluctance of Pygmies to show their identity goes back centuries. Whenever Pygmies have come out of the forest they have tried to hide their identity to get acceptance. Every time someone has tried to make them equal it has only made things worse, like when Mobutu made us citizens and everyone turned this into a joke against us. Being a Pygmy activist seemed a lonely job.

However, I listened to Kabungulu. By the mid 1990s Mobutu's power had weakened a lot. We were still a bit scared, but were using our European names and had started wearing neckties again – Mobutu had banned neckties because he said they were not

African. We could express our opinions freely, and felt encouraged. On Kabungulu's advice I went to talk to three Pygmy elders living in Bukavu: Kangene, Muley and Nyabyamo. These three men are all related to me and to each other through clan ties. Kangene is like a grandfather or great uncle to me, Muley is his younger brother and Nyabyamo is a distant uncle on my mum's side. At the time Kangene was in his late seventies, and he died only a few years ago in his nineties. Muley is still alive. It was Muley's father-in-law who was attacked by the leopard at night in the forest when he went to the toilet.

Kangene was proud to talk about Pygmies and he told me how from the 1950s he started a campaign to get the colonial authorities to pay attention to us. The Belgians became interested, but other Pygmies were not. As it turns out, the colonial administrator of that area wanted help from Kangene to convince Pygmies to put their children in school, which is why he became interested in us. Only a few Pygmies took up this offer; the rest ran away into the forest. The Belgians made Kangene a teacher because he had had a few years of primary school education, and in those days this was considered a lot. Kangene put his children in school and two of his sons became medical doctors. Nyabyamo also went to about Year 3 in primary school in the 1940s, and a Pygmy family in the neighbouring Kalima Chiefdom sent two of their sons to school. One of these sons went on to study dentistry in Europe, and later returned to Bukavu to practice.

Kangene told me that of all the Pygmies in Congo, the Bunyakiri Pygmies are the most educated. It gives us pride that Kangene and a couple of others went to school when most Bantu did not and Pygmies elsewhere were living in the forest. It was these educated

Pygmies who started the fight for our rights, but back in the 1950s the campaign for rights had to be under the umbrella of the BaTembo. Kangene knew everyone thought Pygmies were inferior to Bantu, and he thought any campaign would be stronger if it was about BaTembo rights – but we came to realise that Bantu and Pygmoid people in the BaTembo tribe would never, ever, accept being publicly identified with Pygmies.

All three elders encouraged me to organise the Pygmy community and get the help from abroad. 'Go ahead,' Kangene said. 'We'll support you.' I felt encouraged and went ahead and contacted their children because I wanted their support as well, and I wanted them to know that I had been talking to their fathers. Their children refused. They were concerned that the more they exposed their identity, the more they'd be exposed to discrimination. I spoke to the Pygmy dentist who told me, 'We are not even recognised as a tribe, so when you say you want to create an association for the rights of the Pygmy, it will only cause us problems.' Everyone who knew Kangene's sons knew they were very proud. They had come up from being Pygmies to get an education, and two had finished university. In the forest everyone was equal and had the same aim and goal: to catch meat. In the city educated Pygmies, or Pygmies who are a bit wealthier, don't like to associate with poor Pygmies and they are not going to work with them or with those still in villages. The educated Pygmies try to hide what they are, and to hide any relationship with other Pygmies.

Kabungulu had known that if he contacted educated Pygmies, such as Kangene's children, about the subject of Pygmy rights it would offend them so he had come to me thinking that I could talk to them instead, because I was educated and well off. But

Kangane's children told me that bringing up the fact that they are Pygmies would bring them down. Kabungulu had given me a United Nations brochure to show them that talked about the rights of indigenous people. They told me that saying Pygmies will have justice is a dream that will never come true. Their refusal disappointed me. Mama still thinks like this too. When I told her I was working on this memoir she was not happy and did not encourage me. 'If we have something to eat,' she told me, 'this is enough. If you tell your story it cannot help. We should just leave it and not talk about it. Being a Pygmy is like a curse from God.'

Eventually, after much persuasion, Muley's daughter, Adolphine, agreed to participate and Nyabyamo's son supported the idea, so we went ahead. I suppose Kabungulu was right about me being able to convince others to join an association! I was different because I took the time to listen to Kabungulu when others didn't. I was open to new ideas. Kabungulu was able to convince me that working collectively was a good idea. He explained that if Pygmies could come together we could have a voice at the local government and provincial levels, although maybe not at the national level. He convinced me that I could help all those Pygmies who hide themselves to be proud of their identity.

Our association was created on 2 July 1996. Mobutu's power was, by then, much weaker and people were not so afraid of organising against him any more, although we were still harassed by the army, police and government officials. We did not know that in a few months the whole regime would fall down.

We gave our association a name in French, the language of all official business in Congo: Action d'Appui Pour la Promotion des Droits de Minorités Autochtones en Afrique Centrale (APDMAC)

The Activist and the Elders.
Clockwise from top-left: Kabungulu (of Héritiers de la Justice), Muley, Kangene and Nyabyamo.

Isaac and Mama (Nakashishi) – Sydney, 2014

Josephine in the vegetable garden, with cassava plants and banana tree – Sydney, 2014

Family portrait before leaving for Australia, Nairobi 2003.
Front row, L-R: Boaz, Montil, Jonathan (Jamaa's son).
Sitting: Josephine, Isaac, Wetekay.
Middle back: Fazili, Bikulo, Abishay, Akili (nephew), Jamaa.
Back row: Zawadi, Deborah, Abner.

Josephine and Isaac in front of their Canley Vale home – Sydney, 2014

Abishay in Year 12 at Merrylands High School – Sydney, 2009

Bikulo and Isaac – Sydney, 2006

The Australian generation – Sydney 2004
L-R: Boaz, Jonathan (grandson) and Montil

– Action to Support the Promotion of Indigenous Minority Rights in Central Africa. We wrote a constitution and on the very first page it states that APDMAC is based on the United Nations' International Convention on the Elimination of All Forms of Racial Discrimination. The goal of APDMAC was to help and support Pygmy and Pygmoid people stand up for their rights. The constitution describes the criteria for being a member of APDMAC. At a general meeting, we had agreed that members should be 100 per cent Pygmy, or Pygmoid – it was going to be an association just for us. The BaTembo know who is a Pygmy, who is Pygmoid and who is Bantu, so we knew who was eligible to become a member. When I told the elders Kangene, Muley and Nyabyamo that we had done this, they were very happy.

We decided to open APDMAC to both Pygmy and Pygmoid people, because Pygmoid people still get called Pygmies even if they had a Pygmy ancestor four generations back. Another reason we opened APDMAC to Pygmoid people is because full-blood Pygmies are in the poorest situation. If we work with Pygmoids, that makes Pygmies proud because we would say that our cousins are helping us. However, if APDMAC relied on Pygmies alone it wouldn't work because the strength of an organisation depends on its economic capacity. Still, all the members of APDMAC were poor and we didn't get any external financial help.

My position in APDMAC was Founder and Coordinator. Sinafasi, a Pygmy from the Mangurejipa Forest in North Kivu, was the Secretary. Another daughter of Muley's, Maya, was Treasurer. In the end we had 31 members, which was less than I had hoped. Some of us put down the names of our children to make the membership list look bigger. But at least the association existed, and we registered it as a non-profit organisation with the government.

Kabungulu encouraged me to meet a lot of people and gave me contacts with some Pygmy organisations in Rwanda and Burundi. Everyone was hopeful that the Forest Peoples Programme in London could help us get recognition for the BaTembo Pygmies and do something for us, and I wrote to them asking for their support.

Even though the elders felt happy, personally I felt some disappointment. I was disappointed at the refusal of the dentist and of Kangene's children to join the association. They had good positions in society in Bukavu and I had been counting on their support, but people did not know they were Pygmies, and that is what stopped them joining.

We really owed all of this to Kabungulu. We say he is a *pierre angulaire* – a cornerstone – because he was the first to advocate for Pygmies and did everything to help Pygmies talk for themselves. Kabungulu wanted Pygmies to make their own structure and organisation and then help them with ideas and connections.

One of the first things we did at APDMAC was try to write a history of Pygmies and the BaTembo. We looked in some books written by Belgians about BaTembo people but there wasn't much. The Belgians were interested in Bantu because they wanted labour, but it was hard to catch Pygmies because we kept running away into the forest so they were not very interested in us. The Belgians may have ignored us but Bantu had lots of stereotypes about us and through APDMAC we hoped that we could counter those stereotypes and therefore improve how we were viewed and treated by society.

17

Cadavers from Tchambutsha

While we were organising APDMAC, the new Tutsi-dominated government next door in Rwanda was organising a campaign to overthrow Mobutu. The Rwandan government wanted to get rid of the refugee camps in Congo because they were a mix of civilians and Hutu soldiers from the former Rwandan army who had fought against the Tutsis. The new Rwandan government knew that Mobutu's army was very corrupt and without discipline, and could not fight or control the refugee camps. It also knew that Mobutu was weakened by prostate cancer and was going to die.

The Tutsi government took advantage of Mobutu's weakness and the chaos in Eastern Congo, and found a Congolese – Laurent Kabila – to head an 'Alliance of Democratic Forces for the Liberation of Congo'. The Congolese who joined the Alliance thought it was a good opportunity to get power, while the Rwandan government thought it was a good opportunity to get rid of the Rwandan Hutus sheltering in Congo.

From mid 1996 Congolese Tutsis in South Kivu started mobilising against Mobutu's forces. Then in the early afternoon of 29 October 1996, Alliance soldiers invaded Bukavu from Rwanda and captured the city. Josephine and the children had left two days earlier because we felt something bad was going to happen, but I was still there. Mortars suddenly started coming in from across the river, from Rwanda, and exploding – boom, boom – and blowing up buildings. Alliance forces moved right into Bukavu and took control, and started attacking the refugee camps around the city where hundreds of thousands of Hutus were living.

I ran, along with all the other civilians who were left in town and all the refugees from the camps. We fled up the road that leads to Bunyakiri and then on to Kisangani. Josephine and I reunited in Bunyakiri and we stayed at her brother's place for two weeks, waiting.

Mobutu's soldiers, who were running away, also fled to Bunyakiri. They had not been paid for years, had few weapons and could not even collect much money from the population any more because everyone was poor. Congolese soldiers were not interested in fighting against the Alliance but were not motivated to fight for it either. They took everything from us: our blankets, cooking utensils, bags and clothing, and I had some drugs from my pharmacy that they took as well. The soldiers forced Josephine's nephew to carry all the stuff they had stolen from us and continued to retreat on foot along the road to Kisangani. After 20 kilometres they released him and got someone else from the next village to carry everything.

Josephine's brother was married to a Congolese Tutsi, and after Bukavu was captured his sons and father-in-law were taken by the retreating Congolese army. We managed to locate the army unit that was holding them. They were tied up, ready to be executed. The soldiers were saying, 'You Tutsis came here to kill us, so we are going to kill you!' They thought any Tutsis must be on the side of the Alliance. We begged for their lives. We lied and said that because they spoke KiTembo they could not possibly be Tutsis because Tutsis speak Kinyarwanda. We, ourselves, were then accused of being traitors. However we insisted they were not Tutsis and the soldiers eventually agreed to let them go if we paid them some money. We collected $320 and gave this to the soldiers, who released them. Josephine's brother's Tutsi family members hid in the forest for months after that.

The Alliance's attack started in the east and then some forces went west, some went south and some went north-west – to Kisangani in the middle of the country. From Kisangani they could travel by boat down the Congo River and capture the capital, Kinshasa. But to get there they had to travel along the road through Bunyakiri – where we were.

It was difficult for the Alliance to progress through Bunyakiri because BaTembo and some Hunde started to fight against them. They thought the Alliance was coming to take over their country. Guns were illegal under Mobutu, but if you lived in the forest you were allowed to have a hunting gun and many men had a *calibre-douze*, a twelve-gauge shotgun, paid to them as a bride-price for their daughters. So there were a lot of guns in the forest; every family had one, and the people in the forest around Bunyakiri were mostly BaTembo.

The BaTembo, and people elsewhere, had created small militias known as Mai Mai, some of which had opposed Mobutu's regime for years. The Mai Mai had their *calibre-douze* and sometimes bow and arrows, and they relied on magic to guide and protect them. Laurent Kabila, the leader of the Alliance, was very smart about the Mai Mai. He wanted to make a deal with them so Alliance troops could keep advancing, but the Mai Mai did not like or trust foreigners. Mai Mai and other Congolese were suspicious that Tutsis from Rwanda had a dream of hegemony; they had already taken control of Rwanda and we worried that they wanted to take over Congo as well. Kabila denied this, saying the Alliance could not use Congolese soldiers against Mobutu because they were so poor and had to use foreigners instead, saying they would only be in Congo for a short time. We eventually learnt this was a lie.

Kabila knew that the Mai Mai could not defeat the Alliance, but they were bothering it like mosquitoes. They would attack and kill three or four soldiers, then run away into the forest. Kabila told the Mai Mai that instead of fighting the forces of the Alliance, they should form a common force to chase Mobutu out. Some Mai Mai members signed an accord with the Alliance but others refused and continued to oppose it, and still others said that while they would not fight the Alliance they would stay to protect their villages in case they were attacked. Because of Kabila's accord with Mai Mai groups, the way from Bukavu to Kisangani opened up and the Alliance was able to advance into the interior of Congo.

We heard that Dr George, my Hutu friend from Rwanda who had treated the lump on Josephine's breast, was stuck in a village called Tchambutsha. Tchambutsha was about 50 kilometres from Bunyakiri, towards Kisangani. The road in that area followed the Luo'o River and at Tchambutsha there was a bridge that crossed the river and divided the village into two. Like all the other Hutus fleeing the Alliance, Dr George was worried he would be killed by Alliance soldiers. When I heard he was in Tchambutsha I went there to find him, to save his life. Because I knew the area well, I thought I could get Dr George and his wife and child out, and hide them from Alliance troops in the Kasachi Forest.

I did not find Dr George, but I did find a man I knew called Kamanzi, a Rwandan Hutu businessman. His wife was a Tutsi and they had two sons, one six and one eight years old. They fled to Bukavu during the 1994 genocide, worried that his wife would be killed by génocidaires. But when the Alliance invaded Congo, Kamanzi and his family fled from Bukavu, this time worried that *he* would be killed by Rwandan Tutsis in the Alliance. Along the way, Kamanzi's wife had fallen into a hole and twisted her leg and couldn't walk. She was also slow because she was pregnant with their third child, so Kamanzi left her behind. He knew that if he was to survive he had to keep running with his sons, but he was not too worried about his wife because he thought that when Alliance soldiers saw her they would know she was a Tutsi and would not shoot her.

When I met him in Tchambutsha, Kamanzi was desperate. His two little boys could not walk very fast so they could not keep running together. He told me, 'Isaac, the help you were going to give to Dr George, please give it to me. I'll leave my two kids in your hands and if their mum is not dead you can find her and give them back to her. Just take them as your children.' He asked me to take them to the forest.

Kamanzi didn't have any money because he'd left everything in a hurry. However, in Bukavu he had a new Toyota Corolla and he gave me all the registration documents for the car. I gave him $400. I had more money but I wanted to keep some to help Dr George if I found him. Kamanzi knew Dr George and had seen him along the route. He told me that Dr George would probably arrive in Tchambutsha in the next few days.

Lots of other Hutu kept arriving in Tchambutsha. The Alliance had announced that food and help for genuine Hutu refugees – not génocidaires – would be available in the village. They told people that trucks would be available to take them back to Bukavu and then Rwanda, so they could go home. People gathered there hoping for help, although a few who were suspicious of Alliance forces kept moving on. One girl, who was about seventeen, arrived. She had been bitten by a snake along the route and was crying, asking if anyone could help her get the venom out. No-one could help her so she walked on, but I remember thinking that after a short while the poison would reach her heart and she would die.

Before Dr George arrived, when there were about two thousand refugees gathered, the Tchambutsha massacre began. It was in the morning around seven-thirty or eight o'clock. We heard grenades exploding and Alliance troops started shooting at the refugees. Men, women and children, there was no distinction. All of them were killed. I was 500 metres away, over the bridge and across the river from the village when the killing started, and I heard the gunfire: bup-bup-bup-bup-bup-bup-bup.

People were screaming and running into the river where they drowned. All the Congolese villagers ran away as well. Alliance troops did not touch the Congolese, but after the massacre they forced the young men from Tchambutsha to dump the bodies into the river. I, along with other people, fled into the forest. I took Kamanzi's boys with me. I did not want to bury those dead people.

We ran along the path that comes into Tchambutsha from Goma, but there we met other Hutus coming from Goma who told us to go back because there were more Alliance soldiers behind *them*. Basically, the Alliance was trying to catch the refugees by trapping them from two directions. It was a crazy time. There were a few Hutus who managed to escape with us. In the villages where Hutus took shelter, Congolese boys started raping the Hutu girls.

Village chiefs tried to stop it, worried that such behaviour would bring a curse on the village. They managed to stop some rapes, but still, there were a lot.

In the forest people looked for big trees to shelter under or built shelters out of branches and leaves. I joined a group of about thirty Congolese. They had two or three tarpaulins they had hung up between trees, and they let us sleep under them. After talking to them we worked out that some were from the same clan as Josephine and had also fled into the forest to escape the fighting. 'Those two kids are Rwandan; how come you have them?' they asked. I explained that their father was a friend of mine and had had to run away. I was not comfortable in the forest because I had become habituated to urban life, but I knew that the forest would be safe until Alliance forces had moved on. We went to the river looking for crabs and fish, and some people went to abandoned fields around Tchambutsha to collect cassava and bananas.

Other Hutus came into our camp to ask for directions. They did not speak Swahili, only Kinyarwanda – the language of Rwanda – so it was difficult for them. I had spoken Kinyarwanda since I was a child on Mr François' farm, mixing with all the Tutsi families that worked there, so I could speak to them. They were all trying to get to Kisangani , to a refugee camp called Tingi-Tingi that they heard the Red Cross had established. We were scared these Hutus were going to kill us because some of them had guns and they were feeling wrathful because of what was happening.

After a few days in the forest the old men sent young boys to Tchambutsha to see if all the dead people had been put in the river. We thought that the Alliance would not waste time staying in the area but would keep advancing towards the big cities like

Kisangani. The young boys discovered the Alliance forces had moved on, and villagers started to return to Tchambutsha.

I went back after about ten days in the forest. As we approached Tchambutsha we saw dead people who had not been buried lying in the grass beside the path, and there was a terrible smell. We only looked at them for a few seconds. I remember one man was covered with flies that were eating him. Another was lying on his back with his mouth open and his fingers like stiff claws, and he had a small black bag dropped beside him.

The village chief was worried about the dead causing disease and got people to bury the bodies that were left. But I, Kamanzi's two boys and a Congolese woman with twins about five years old, left to walk the 50 kilometres to Bunyakiri. The woman was actually the twins' aunt. They had become separated from their mother, and she was looking after them.

It was a terrible walk to Bunyakiri. We were all exhausted and the children could only walk very slowly. That afternoon I suddenly saw one of Josephine's nephews, Katindi, coming towards me. Josephine's family had heard that I had been killed in the Tchambutsha massacre. In our culture we cannot commence our six days of mourning for someone who has died until we have seen the body, so they had sent Katindi to Tchambutsha to find my body and confirm my death. Katindi could not believe I was alive. He joined our party but we had to spend that night by the roadside because we could not go the whole way in one day.

The next day we walked into Bunyakiri. When people saw me they said, 'I don't believe I'm seeing you! You and your friend were killed together in Tchambutsha!' Everyone had heard about the massacre. I explained that the killing had started before

Dr George had arrived and that I had run away into the forest. I went to Josephine's family's house, and they told me that she and the children had already returned to Bukavu. Someone brought twelve bottles of Primus beer to celebrate me being alive. I got drunk that night.

We had to stay in Bunyakiri for Christmas as we waited to find transport back to Bukavu. I had bad images in my head from the massacre. There was also no way to communicate with Josephine because there were no working phone lines, so she knew nothing about me being alive. We stayed for a week and on 5 January finally got a truck to Bukavu and I went home.

Josephine was jumping on me! Pressing me and squashing me. All the kids surrounded me, hanging on to my legs and grabbing my hands. Each one wanted to hold a part of me. Everybody was talking with emotion and the children were crying. The neighbours came to see me that evening, and my friends started to hear that I had turned up alive in Bukavu. For a week I received visitors.

For me there was a mix of joy and pain. I was so happy to see Josephine and the children again, but a new regime run by the Alliance and Rwandans now ruled Bukavu. The new regime had also taken my three vehicles. A lot of people had been killed, even rich people. I heard of one Congolese who had been killed with his wife and all his children. I consoled myself that at least I was alive and that losing my vehicles was nothing, but even now, here in Australia, sometimes cadavers from Tchambutsha come to me in my dreams.

Kamanzi's sons stayed with us in Bukavu for a few weeks. I eventually tracked down their mother in Cyangugu, just over the border from Bukavu. I had never really worried about her safety because she was a Tutsi. The border with Rwanda had re-opened and I took the boys back to their mother. She was very happy and crying – tender motherly emotion. The boys grabbed her legs and waist, hanging on to her, hugging and crying. Her husband, Kamanzi, was not there – I found out later that he had been killed – and I could tell that despite being reunited with her boys there was grief in her heart. She had also given birth. That new baby would never know its daddy.

With the registration papers Kamanzi had given me, I went to collect his Toyota Corolla. I discovered that a Métis, a Greek Congolese, was driving the car around Bukavu. He had been appointed to a senior position in the new rebel administration that now governed Bukavu. He thought he could just steal the property of anyone who had left. I explained that I had bought the car from a Hutu who had run away, and showed him my registration papers. I also fabricated a receipt that said I had bought the car before the war started. If he knew I'd never actually had the car in my possession he would not have given it to me. The Métis kept refusing, and I was in a difficult position because he was very powerful amongst the rebel forces who now controlled the city. I went to a magistrate to try to get help through the courts but he told me, 'There is no court now. We are powerless. You had better go to see the Métis' boss and complain to him.' I went to see the boss, a Tutsi. I took Kamanzi's sons with me and got them to say that I had bought the car before the war. The boss told the Métis 'We are trying to create a regime different to Mobutu. You have to give back the car.' He did, but before he gave it back he took the radio, the tyres and the battery.

But the story does not stop there. Kamanzi's wife came to me after I had the car and said, 'I know you saved the life of my kids, but the $400 you gave my husband for the car cannot buy another car. I don't want someone to take the car from you, but I'd like you to give me another $2000.' People told me to be careful, reminding me that she was a Tutsi and Tutsis were in power now in Bukavu through the Alliance. They warned me that she might have me killed if I didn't give her money. But I argued with her, telling her, 'Even your words would not get the car back from the Alliance regime. I got it back because I had the documents.' She explained that she was in a hard financial situation and thought her only hope to earn money was to get back the car and then sell it.

In the end I gave her $1000 but I was upset about this and thought she was ungrateful. I had taken her boys into the forest, walked with them from Tchambutsha to Bunyakiri, and looked after them in my house in Bukavu. I think life is full of horrible things and people have different personalities, and this comes out in the way they cope. There are those who are grateful, those who are ungrateful; those who are sensitive, those who are insensitive; there are caring people and those who don't care.

18

Moni stands up

After the Alliance conquered Congo, there was a period of calm when Laurent Kabila became our new president. Kabila was sharp. When he took power he tried to make changes, and he put Rwandans in charge because he didn't trust Congolese to make reforms. But changing the entire system is very, very difficult. All the wrongdoers claimed Kabila wanted foreigners to make laws in the country, while others complained their salaries were not enough. They said these things to try to stop the reforms.

The people liked Kabila because he put his ministers in prison if they were corrupt, but he was a dictator and had bad habits. He wanted to take all the power himself and not distribute it to his ministers or advisers, and he was a glutton for women and wanted all the beautiful women of Kinshasa to become his.

Congolese had been tired of Mobutu and were happy to see him go, but we were also fed up with all the Rwandans who came to our country after the genocide and wanted them to go back home. Then we saw that the Alliance was full of Rwandan Tutsis and not Congolese. The Alliance had seemed like a good thing, but it quickly became clear it was controlled by Rwandans and we told each other, 'We're going to be a Rwandan colony.'

In Bukavu, the Rwandan military used to get into taxis and tell the drivers to take them around town, without any payment. The drivers eventually refused to do this, so the Rwandans forced them out of their cars, made them lie on the side of the road, and beat them. The Rwandans had a low opinion of Congolese and used to joke that we were BMWs, like the car: we only cared about Beer, Music and Women. Soldiers also used to occasionally spit on people to show us we were nothing. When Kabila made a Rwandan Tutsi head of the Congolese army, Congolese did not like it and all the Mai Mai militias turned against Kabila.

Instead of leaving Congo now that Mobutu had been chased out, Tutsis who came with the Alliance were left to govern the areas they had conquered. Congolese were forced to accept them as part of society, and we felt we were under occupation. So despite hating the Mobutu regime, people did not welcome the Alliance and resisted it. Opportunists joined the new regime because they knew they could get power if they supported it.

Some Tutsis found it difficult to believe that they had taken over Central Africa. There is a passage in the Bible, in Isaiah Chapter 60 that says, 'A little one shall become a thousand, and a small one a strong nation.' Once they got over the surprise, people started interpreting this passage as a prophecy about Tutsis and Rwanda, a very small country, becoming a powerful nation.

Some Rwandans had come to Congo during the colonial period but many more, especially Tutsis, came as refugees after 1959 and 1960, when Rwanda got independence and Hutus took control. A lot of Congolese viewed the Tutsis in Congo as refugees, so if you were a Tutsi you tried to disguise your identity because refugees were not considered normal citizens. These Tutsis who had been hiding their identity became excited when Tutsis became powerful in the new regime in Congo, and they started to reveal their identity. Congolese did not understand how Tutsis, who had come as refugees, had ended up being their rulers. This was shocking.

In 1997, my old neighbour and pharmaceuticals selling agent, Moni, stood up. Moni had been my close friend for a long time but I did not know he was a Tutsi until the Alliance took power. Everyone thought he was from the Shi tribe. He had come to Bunyakiri as a teacher when he was a young man, married a local girl, a Rega, then the Alliance came and put him in charge of the whole Bunyakiri area! All the Tutsis became Moni's friends when he got power. The Alliance gave him a 250cc motorcycle, bodyguards and weapons. People had known Moni for years but he changed completely after he got this position. He wore two pistols on his hips when he walked around Bunyakiri, just like a cowboy, and he started to show off and killed a lot of people.

Moni had been irritated by the Mai Mai militias blocking the Alliance's advance until it signed an accord with them. Once the accord was signed and the officers and Alliance forces had continued on to Kisangani, Moni began to take revenge. A lot of teenagers in Bunyakiri had joined Mai Mai militias. Those whose militias joined with the Alliance advanced on to Kisangani and other cities, leaving their families behind. Moni went to those families and started to persecute them. He told them, 'You, your son was going to fight the Alliance in the forest if we did not sign an accord. Where is your son today?' He asked for money or palm oil and put people in prison if they did not pay up. There were some Mai Mai that had refused to join the Alliance, who had simply returned to their families but were not participating in fighting. Moni started killing them. He had them shot and their bodies thrown into the Luo'o River. 'God is in Heaven and I am God here in Bunyakiri,' he declared.

Moni even humiliated a good friend of his, Makelele. Moni and Makelele were Jehovah's Witnesses, and Makelele was from the BaTembo tribe like me. Part of Jehovah's Witness dogma is that God is the only one who can make a judgement, not a human. Jehovah's Witnesses do not punish anyone, they do not take sides in conflicts and they do not kill other human beings. During the Rwandan genocide the Hutu government told the people to 'defend the country' – this meant kill Tutsis – but Hutus and Tutsis who were Jehovah's Witnesses never killed. Jehovah's Witnesses should never kneel down before another human being, such as priests, or before images, like Jesus on the Cross or the Virgin. A Jehovah's Witness only kneels before God and by that they mean Jehovah, the God from the Jewish Bible and the Old Testament. Not Jesus.

When the Jehovah's Witness congregation in Bunyakiri saw Moni become so political and take up weapons Makelele, as an Elder in the congregation, tried to counsel him. This had no impact on Moni, who continued to order killings. Makelele and some others went to Moni's house and gathered on his verandah to talk to him. I suppose they wanted to remind him of the Jehovah's Witness teachings – and expel him from the congregation if he did not stop what he was doing. Moni started to ask Makelele: 'So, Jehovah is God in Heaven, but who is God here? I am God here! Kneel in front me!' Moni knew that Makelele should not do that. Could not do that. 'Your life is in my hands,' Moni said. 'I am the god here on Earth and I will see if Jehovah will help you! If you want to live, you have to kneel!' Makelele knew he was finished. Moni had already arranged the killing of other people. He begged for forgiveness and bent a little bit, but Moni ordered him to put his knees on the ground.

I still cannot believe that Moni made Makelele kneel. This story went around all Bunyakiri and when I heard it, I became afraid of Moni. Moni owed me $500. Before the Alliance's invasion he had bought medicine worth $1500 from my pharmacy in Bukavu. He paid $1000 and promised to pay the rest later. After Mobutu's regime fell I wanted to ask Moni for my $500, but I became afraid and didn't.

When Moni started killing Mai Mai, they in return started planning to kill him. There was still a lot of conflict in Eastern Congo and one day Moni's Tutsi bodyguards were called away by the Alliance troops. Moni was without support for about two days, and the Mai Mai knew this. Moni felt insecure and got on his motorbike to ride to Bukavu, which was safer for him. On the way he came across a roadblock set up by a Mai Mai militia made up of child soldiers, called *kadogo* in Swahili. When they saw Moni they said, 'Our commander wants to talk to you.' Moni was not a soldier himself and he was outnumbered so he was not going to fight them. They took his weapons and a *kadogo* got on the motorbike behind Moni and put a gun in his back. When they reached the Luo'o River, the *kadogo* told him to cross and wait on the other side. Moni reached the other side and the *kadogo* shot him in the head.

Moni was tall, and a very big man. The *kadogo* wasn't strong enough to dispose of the body himself, but there was a woman nearby out looking for firewood and she had seen everything – this is how we found out what happened. The *kadogo* forced her to help him throw Moni into the river. Moni's body got stuck in the branches of a dead tree in the middle of the river and a cloud of butterflies came to pick at him. People started a song, called *Moni's song*, to tell the story of his death.

Don't be like Moni, because God rejected him.
Even Satan has rejected him.
The Luo'o River has refused to take him.
Which side – Heaven or Hell – is he going to stay?

This song went around the whole Bunyakiri district and by hearing it and singing it everyone learnt what had happened to Moni. It made us think about him being stuck for eternity in the middle of nowhere.

The same day, the Mai Mai went to Moni's home. They searched his house and found his wife and children. When they tried to resist, the Mai Mai said, 'Do you want us to take you where we took your father?' Moni's wife and son had thought Moni had gone to Bukavu, but when they heard this they realised Moni was dead and let the Mai Mai search the house. So many weapons were taken from his house: pistols and M16 and AK47 machine guns. Some of the *kadogo* wanted to rape Moni's wife, but other *kadogo* believed that if they raped their powers to survive and fight would be weakened. Instead, they took all her clothes and left her naked to humiliate her in front of her children.

People were happy Moni was dead. Before the Alliance took power, Moni had been a good man with a good reputation and he had a lot of friends. When the Tutsis took power he changed completely: he became wicked and terrifying. Nobody expected him to change like that. No-one could believe that Moni could give an order to kill someone. I could not believe it either, because it was Moni who had defended me to Josephine's sister after I got married and told her off for criticising me.

People may be good for a long period of time, but I think

behaviour can change according to circumstances. Any human being can change. If a Pygmy became president, all the Pygmies would come out of hiding and rise up just like the Tutsis did. Moni changed negatively. Instead of helping friends, he started intimidating and killing people. He was overexcited by the power he gained. I concluded that an invisible force must have driven Moni to become so wicked. A normal person could not act like that.

19

Occupation

Laurent Kabila had become President of Congo but there was a lot of pressure on him. Rwanda and Uganda wanted to be in full control. They wanted Kabila to be a marionette, a puppet, someone who was there as president but implementing their decisions rather than his own, as they were the ones who'd given him the power he now had. Kabila was very proud but did not accept that Ugandans and Rwandans were also very proud. There was also pressure against Kabila from Congolese because he was using foreigners to run the country. A lot of top positions in Kabila's government were filled by Rwandans.

It became hard for Kabila to manage the Alliance. He said all the foreign armies should return to their countries, and told them to leave. Rwanda and Uganda did not accept this and started a second war against him, this time under the name Le Rassemblement Congolais pour la Démocratie – the Congolese Rally for Democracy, or RCD. They took some Congolese and put them in public positions in the RCD to try to give themselves a Congolese cover, but it was really mostly made up of Ugandans and Tutsi Rwandans. This started a big war between the RCD, Uganda and Rwanda on one side, and President Kabila, who got support from Zimbabwe, Angola, Namibia, Sudan and Chad. Lots of the Mai Mai militias in the east also supported Kabila. So from 1998 to 2003 Congo became divided: the east was occupied by RCD rebel forces and its foreign supporters, and the west by government forces and its foreign supporters – foreigners on both sides. When the RCD rebels created a new regime to govern Eastern Congo, including Bukavu, people knew it was a Rwandan occupation and not a true Congolese government and became hostile to it.

Life in Bukavu under the RCD was hard. There were no flights east to west, or from Rwanda or Uganda to Kinshasa. People could go to Dar es Salaam in Tanzania and then fly to Kinshasa but it was very expensive. People living in Bukavu who were from Kinshasa or Lubumbashi, which were in government-held areas, were stuck. They could not go back and it was difficult for them to communicate with their families. If they did go back they were suspected by the Kabila government of being spies, because they had just come from areas occupied by anti-government forces.

A lot of people living in RCD-controlled areas were taken from their homes. Some Congolese became paid informers for the RCD regime and betrayed Hutus who tried to hide amongst the Congolese. Those Hutus then disappeared. If you said something against the RCD rebels they would put you in prison if you were lucky, but mostly, you just disappeared at night. People who had an unresolved problem amongst themselves went to the rebel regime and said, 'That person supports the Mai Mai!' just to get revenge. It was like under Mobutu, but back then they did it to take your money, not to have you killed. If people knew someone dealt with the RCD regime everyone became scared of them. There was so much suspicion about each other and wondering about who was a collaborator. People had no trust.

There were also shortages. In Bukavu and Goma there was a lack of palm oil, used for cooking and to make soap, because it came from the countryside which was controlled by Mai Mai militias who were against the rebel regime. Traders were scared to travel to the countryside, to places like Bunyakiri, to buy it. There was a lack of cassava and cassava flour, the staple food in Congo, because it was also grown in Mai Mai areas. Traders who transported food, soap and clothing through the forest were considered by the rebel regime to be helping the Mai Mai – to be taking supplies to the Mai Mai, as well as information about the rebels – so the regime killed them. The population of Bukavu swelled to about one million because of people fleeing into town from the countryside to avoid fighting, but there was a shortage of food and many people lacked money to buy anything. We listened to the BBC, Voice of America and Radio France Internationale for news, because local television in Goma and Bukavu was just rebel propaganda. It was a really hard time.

In terms of safety, my family was a bit safe in Bukavu because the RCD was totally in control there so there was no fighting. However, in Bunyakiri and the countryside there was constant conflict between Mai Mai militias and rebel forces. The rebel regime really only ruled in Bukavu and Goma. There was a famous Mai Mai leader called Padiri, which means priest in Swahili. He was a very good leader and we heard stories about his success in fighting the rebels. When his militia caught Congolese who were fighting for the rebel regime, he said, 'They are our friends and brothers. Even if they fight for money, don't harm them.' He forgave them – like a priest – and that is where his name came from. People supported the Mai Mai, but not openly. After a battle the Mai Mai often disappeared into the homes of people to hide. The population, because it was against the rebel regime, was ready to help them. It saw the Mai Mai as saviours against Rwandan and Tutsi domination.

In 1999 the Mai Mai came out of the forest to attack rebel troops in Bunyakiri. They attacked the hotel where soldiers were sleeping. The rebels said everyone in Bunyakiri was related to the Mai Mai – their mother or their cousin – and was supporting them, and began to take revenge. At five o'clock in the morning rebel forces came to kill people in their houses who they suspected of supporting the Mai Mai. They killed about twenty. Not with pistols or bullets, but with knives. People heard the cries of victims and started to flee their homes.

That year the rebels burnt down a lot of houses in Bunyakiri. They detained a lot of men, including Tschambu, the pharmacist I had employed at my Bunyakiri pharmacy. The rebels made them lie on their backs on the road in Bunyakiri town centre, facing up towards the sun. They made them look straight into the sun and if you blinked, they beat you. Soldiers stood either side of the row of men looking for those who were blinking. At the end of the day, when they released them, all the men were half-blind. Tschambu became completely blind and he stayed blind until he died in 2006.

When these things happened the world did nothing – just like in Rwanda during the genocide when neighbours killed each other with machetes. Or Tchambutsha. The massacre was like in the movies, but it was real. There was no reaction from those who are supposed to protect people in the world. They just ignored it. After the peace agreement that ended the war in 2002, the people who did these atrocities eventually went into power in the Congolese government … and then talked about human rights!

The RCD occupation and the division of Congo were bad for the pharmaceutical business. People had run away from their homes and had less money than before. When the rebels burnt down houses in Bunyakiri they set fire to my pharmacy as well, after taking all the drugs, which they claimed helped the Mai Mai. Because of the difficulty travelling between Bukavu and Bunyakiri, I could not supply the pharmacy very well even if I had rebuilt it, so I closed it. I had already closed my Minova pharmacy near Goma because there was too much insecurity with soldiers in the town and Mai Mai all around. Even business at the pharmacy in Bukavu started to collapse because most of my customers were from the countryside, and it was no longer safe for them to travel to Bukavu. Some of my customers had come from Katanga province to the south, but that area was now controlled by government forces and flights to Bukavu had stopped. I needed a new business.

The only people making money during that time were those dealing in a mineral called coltan, which is used in hi-tech electronics such as mobile phones, iPads and laptops. The Mai Mai controlled areas where it was mined. We had never heard of coltan before about 1999, but suddenly people everywhere were talking about it and trying to get it because there was a price boom as buyers tried to obtain as much coltan as possible for those new gadgets. People dug new mines using primitive methods, and when they found coltan other people rushed into the area. There were small mines all over the forest and the miners wanted consumer goods. People started to take every risk and carried goods like salt, soap, dried fish, shoes and clothing into the Mai Mai areas to the mines. The miners paid for their goods in cash or in coltan itself. The traders risked punishment from rebel forces, but they needed to survive.

The rebel regime wanted to control the coltan trade because it was so lucrative, but the Mai Mai controlled the mines. If the rebels stopped the traders the coltan wouldn't come out from the forest, so they eventually tried to find a way to allow the trade. They eased restrictions so people could bring coltan into Bukavu and Goma, where it was bought by business people working for the regime. The regime then made money by controlling its export. I saw that the people who were doing coltan business with the RCD regime had changed their lives.

I was on a business trip to Kampala, the capital of Uganda, to buy pharmaceuticals for the Bukavu pharmacy when I met a Congolese who told me there were European people in Uganda looking for coltan, and that if I could supply it they were ready to finance me. 'If you are interested, I can introduce you to one of the Europeans,' he said. You need a lot of capital to trade in coltan because normally you need an entire container for export. One shipping container can hold 20 tonnes of coltan, so that means you need a lot of money to buy this much, and I did not have this kind of money. That made obtaining finance in advance very important.

This man took me to the office of an Englishman, Mr Brookes. He had a very nice office in the centre of Kampala, with several people working there, and it seemed to be a reputable business. Mr Brookes told me that if I could supply him with coltan we could make good business. He said he needed at least a tonne and couldn't give me money in advance the first time. However, if I could bring him a tonne, the next time he could give me money to buy 10 tonnes – half a shipping container. I felt happy to have found a business partner.

I sold one of my houses in Bukavu for $27,000 to obtain enough capital to buy a 1.3 tonne consignment of coltan, and I transported the shipment to Kampala. The coltan was kept at a warehouse until its mineral content had been determined, a process that would take a few weeks as Mr Brookes said the samples would be sent to London. It was important to know the exact mineral content of the shipment because that is what determines the price. Because Mr Brookes was British, I thought everything would be okay, but while he was waiting to hear about the results of the mineral content test he secretly shipped the coltan to Britain. I was left with no coltan and no payment.

I thought *muzungus*, white men, were honest and rich! Like Tutsis, their degree of honesty is high compared to Congolese. If a white man promises to pay you $1000, he will. They respect time and contracts. But it does not mean there are no crooks amongst them. I discovered that *muzungus* will also cheat when big money is involved, whereas a rich Congolese will cheat you even if it involves $50.

I was stuck in Kampala. I needed to get my money so did not want to leave, but I didn't know anyone. I went to the police chief in Kampala about my problem. When I told him my story he wanted to arrest Mr Brookes. The police chief told Mr Brookes that he had to return my coltan or pay me the money, but Mr Brookes went to the British Embassy. The embassy spoke to the Ugandan President, who said it was a civil matter and Mr Brookes should not be imprisoned, so he was released. He then escaped Uganda and fled back to Britain.

I stayed in Kampala and went to Interpol to complain. They asked for administrative costs for lodging my application – a genuine fee, not a bribe – but I had no money left. They agreed to take down the details anyway but warned it would take me longer. They found that Englishman in London – from Uganda! They told Mr Brookes that he had to return my money.

While I was staying in Kampala I had become friendly with someone with connections to the Ugandan Foreign Minister. This friend took up the matter with the minister, who somehow agreed to help. I'm not sure what he did, but after six months the minister's wife herself phoned me and told me Mr Brookes wanted to pay me $11,000 to settle the case. He actually owed me $27,000, so I was not happy about this. 'This British man is a crook,' she told me. 'Just take the $11,000 if that is what you can get.' I took the money and offered her $1000 as a gift to say thank you for her help. She refused! 'You have been suffering for a long time and need that money,' she said. I protested and said she had helped me so much, but she still refused. A Congolese minister or minister's wife would never do this. He or she would go to Mr Brookes, take the coltan from him and sell it, or propose to split it with him.

It took me ten months to get any return from that coltan and I lost a house as well, but with the money I got back from Mr Brookes I bought some land in Bukavu where I eventually built a new house.

20

Then you disappear

During the occupation by the rebel regime we were still going on with APDMAC, but it was difficult. You can't talk about human rights during war. We could only reach those Pygmies living in Bukavu and close to the Kahuzi-Biéga National Park, which was also controlled by rebel forces. Most pygmies lived in areas controlled by the Mai Mai so it was very hard to communicate with them.

The owners of the forest became those who had guns. If APDMAC went there and said, 'Pygmies are the owners of the forest,' they would put us in prison. In the past, Pygmies did not worry about the future. Life was easy because it was easy to find something to eat and there was only one need: meat. There was no need for clothing or chairs or spectacles, just meat. The only difficulty was hunting big animals like wild boar, buffalo and elephants. The war and occupation made Pygmies think. Many had fled deep into the forest because of the fighting but life was hard because militias operated there as well. They might be killed or raped. There was no medicine in the forest and many people died because of this, including my papa. Pygmies started to think about building houses and having a permanent village.

In 1999 Kabungulu arranged for three representatives from APDMAC to attend a workshop in Kigali, Rwanda, about Pygmies of Central Africa. We chose three people to attend. I went as the coordinator and we chose Sinafasi because we wanted to show that

APDMAC was not just for Bunyakiri Pygmies. Kabungulu told us to take a woman as well. We asked Maya, one of our members to come as a representative of the women. She hesitated because it meant saying publicly she was a Pygmy, but she talked to her father about it who told her, 'You are what you are,' and she came.

This workshop was a big experience for me. I met Pygmies from Rwanda and we talked about our common problems: of discrimination, and land, and access to forests. Seeing that other organisations for indigenous people existed really encouraged me. I felt that we were not alone and I felt empowered. At the workshop I met a lady from the Forest Peoples Programme, Dorothy Jackson. Dorothy was in her forties and was short and skinny. She approached things scientifically. She told us that problems can be solved, that we have to face them, talk to those responsible and go to court if necessary.

Dorothy told us about other indigenous people and how they fight for their rights. We heard about the Maasai who were fighting the Kenyan government and international organisations that protect wildlife there. When a lion ate a Maasai's cow the Maasai got a small amount of money in compensation – not enough to buy another cow. But when a Maasai kills a lion to protect his cows, the government sends a helicopter with officials to investigate. Those officials and the petrol to run the helicopter cost so much money! The Maasai who killed the lion would be arrested and put in gaol, but if a lion kills a cow or a person no helicopter comes from Nairobi. The Maasai community came together and complained to the government about this injustice, and things have improved for them.

Sinafasi, Maya and I returned to Bukavu with new ideas. One of the main ones was the importance of including women in

APDMAC, and when we got home we created a women's branch. Dorothy also put us in touch with Survival International, an organisation that works for the rights of tribal people around the world, and Minority Rights Group International, which campaigns for the rights of disadvantaged minorities and indigenous people.

In 1999, Dorothy visited us in Bukavu. We gave her copies of our constitution and complained about Kapupu – the one who called himself the King of the Pygmies. Kapupu was upset at the creation of APDMAC. A representative from his organisation had even told Dorothy that we – the organisers of APDMAC – were not Pygmies, but were Bantu BaTembo. Kapupu did not want Pygmies who had an education or a job to be recognised as Pygmies. He needed Pygmies to be poor and ignorant, then he could give them things and claim he was King.

APDMAC was created to bring Pygmy and Pygmoid people together, but trying to organise and improve things can cause a lot of headache. Pygmies and Pygmoids do not care about working together because acting collectively just brings more humiliation. If you don't have a Pygmy identity you are treated better, so Pygmies do not want to act together as a collective.

In 1999 we got invited to another conference, this time at Makere University in Kampala, organised by the Forest Peoples Programme together with Survival International and Minority Rights Group International. At the conference there was a lot of information about Pygmies from different countries: Congo, Congo-Brazzaville, Rwanda, Burundi and Uganda. Everyone explained the problems of their communities, and Sinafasi and I also spoke. We explained how Pygmies in Congo living close to cities want to cultivate land but are prevented from doing so. We also explained how the Pygmies in the interior of Congo do not have a problem with land because the forest is so big. In the interior, the problem for Pygmies is restrictions on hunting for those living around special areas, like national parks. We heard how Pygmies in Uganda were restricted from hunting in a national park, just like my father had been banned from hunting in the Kahuzi-Biéga National Park, and received no compensation and were given nowhere else to live. There was one speaker from England who talked about Australian Aborigines and how they were oppressed by the coloniser and have the same land problems as Pygmies. We had no idea about Australia or Aborigines. I knew that there were black people in India but was surprised to learn they were in Australia as well.

I went to another conference in Bujumbura, the capital of Burundi, in 2000. It was on ecosystems and biodiversity and the President of Burundi chaired the conference. I met a lot of government ministers from different countries and delegations from overseas. They wanted Pygmies involved in the conference because they knew that Pygmies have protected the forest for years. Pygmies make a bit of charcoal or chop a bit of wood to sell, but Bantu bring machines and cut down the whole forest. When hunting, Pygmies kill one animal. Bantu use guns and kill twenty. Minority Rights Group then organised for me to attend another conference in 2001, the United Nations World Conference Against Racism in Durban, South Africa. This was going to be a huge conference with thousands of people, and I was excited. Minority Rights Group sent me information about the conference themes and told me to prepare a speech. I was going to talk about how the dominant tribes bring down the Pygmies and never listen to them, and how Pygmies try to hide their real identity because of discrimination. I spent one or two weeks getting my documents ready, and on Thursday 28 December 2000 went to immigration to lodge my passport and request exit papers. Because of the war, there were tight controls on movement out of the country, so I had to get permission to leave Congo to attend the conference in advance.

That night, at 8 pm, two soldiers came to my house and arrested me. I was surprised. I had thought that if I was going to have trouble getting my exit papers to go to Durban they would have asked me questions when I got to immigration. Instead, they came just after dinner and took me away. They asked, 'Who is oppressing Pygmies? Who is oppressing you? Can you name one Pygmy who has been arrested or tortured?' I was put in a dark, dirty, windowless cell with just me inside. I saw other cells next to mine but I didn't know who was in them.

I had bad memories of being arrested in 1986. After 1998 all government agencies had come under the control of the RCD rebel regime, which we all knew meant under the control of the Rwandan military. The regime was killing anyone suspected of criticising them. A lot of innocent people were killed before any investigation was done as to whether they really had said something bad about the RCD. I was scared of the rebels but I was even more scared of the Rwandan authorities.

Josephine was so worried. She went to see the provincial commander of the army, who was a distant relative of hers, and asked for help. He arranged for me to be brought to him from my cell and told me, 'Already the Rwandan authorities have put a question mark next to you because of what you said in Kigali. There were foreigners from London at the workshop who heard what you said. If you tell something to foreigners it is given high consideration by the rebel regime and Rwandan authorities. What you said gave a bad image of the regime, and it was in front of foreigners. I'm telling you, this is serious.' I didn't realise there had been spies in the workshop and protested that there had been other people from APDMAC there, but the commander told me that I was the leader and this was why I had been arrested. 'Look, we do not have any power,' he said. 'The Rwandans can take you at night from your cell and we cannot stop them. Then you disappear.' He told me that if the rebel regime or Rwandans suspected someone just a little bit, they kill that person. He advised that if I wanted to be safe I needed to get out of rebel territory – to Kinshasa or Lubumbashi – or to leave Congo entirely. The commander agreed to help me and said he would ask the secret police chief if I could be allowed to escape.

The price was $5000. Josephine took the money from our savings and gave it to the commander who split it with the secret police chief. I knew none of this at the time because the commander had spoken separately to Josephine, but that night, on 1 January, a guard came to my cell. He told me a friend had come to see me but I thought, 'What friend comes to a gaol at night?' I didn't want to leave the cell because I thought I was going to be taken away and killed. The commander said, 'I know you don't know what your wife has done, but she gave me some money and I'll try to stop those who could harm you. Go home now, but don't stay at home. I'll be watching out for you.' He drove me home and dropped me off. The soldiers with him didn't know what was going on or that Josephine had paid him.

I got home at about 11 pm and knocked on the door. Josephine was so relieved to see me and quickly let me in. She explained what she had done. All the kids were sleeping, and we sat whispering in the living room. My head was spinning and I couldn't sleep. I didn't know what to do and had to find a solution. Finally, in the middle of the night, I realised I had to leave Congo.

At 5 am, when it was still dark and the kids were sleeping, Josephine and I went to the home of a friend who now worked for the rebel regime as a senior immigration officer. I knew he didn't like the regime and would not harm us. I said I wanted my family to leave Congo and asked him to arrange travel documents for Josephine and the children. Everyone who left with a big family was suspecting of fleeing, so big families were always questioned. We also knew that if I travelled with the family, then it risked us all being arrested. Josephine and the children would have to cross the border without me. The friend told Josephine to look for him at immigration on the border, and he would help them to cross to Cyangugu in Rwanda on the other side.

The same morning I went to see another friend, Marcel. I explained that I didn't have money – we had spent our cash on the bribe to get me out of gaol – but had to leave Congo. I told Marcel that I could not ask for a loan because I didn't know when I could pay it back, and that I also did not have time to sell one of my houses properly. But I told him that if he gave me $25,000 I would give him my two-storey commercial building in Bukavu, where I had my pharmacy shop. It was worth much more than that, perhaps $50,000, but I was desperate. Marcel told me, 'I don't have that much money, but if you could accept $15,000 I can get you the amount straightaway.' He was taking advantage of the situation. I tried to bargain, but he said, 'I don't need a two-storey building, but I need my money' so I had no choice. I couldn't ask someone else to buy the building because I was worried they would start to talk and I would be caught.

That afternoon he gave me the $15,000. I gave $2000 to Josephine and she got the travel documents. We prepared the children and said goodbye. We arranged to meet at a cheap hotel, the Exotic Inn, in Kampala, Uganda, in a few days' time. When Josephine did not return that evening I felt good. I thought they must be safely out.

But I was still in Congo. I heard that people were looking for me, so that night I hid at Marcel's house – he saw that I was in need. Early the next morning I left. I wanted to avoid the border crossing at Bukavu because of all the spies, police and soldiers there. Instead I fled north, hoping to cross directly into Uganda from Congo, bypassing Rwanda. There was police control at the Bukavu harbour where boats go to Goma, so I got a lift on top of a truck travelling the 200 kilometres around Lake Kivu to Goma. The secret police sometimes checked who was staying in hotels, so once in Goma I went to the house of a friend. I didn't tell him what had happened, I just said I was on a business trip to Kampala. I did not want to risk crossing at the Goma–Rwanda border either, so the next morning I took a minibus to Bunagana, a small border crossing to Uganda, 80 kilometres north of Goma.

At the Bunagana border post I went to immigration to get my exit stamp. Two immigration officers started looking at me, questioning me, asking why I was going to Kampala. 'We've never seen you at this border,' they said. I explained I had visited a friend in Goma and was travelling to Kampala for business, but the senior police officer said he suspected me. I thought they must have heard something. In 1997, a colleague of mine, Chika, was travelling into Uganda through another border post at Ishasha, and was carrying $30,000. He imported pharmaceuticals into Congo like me. Chika and his friend were arrested by Alliance police officers, who stole their money, killed them and dumped their bodies in the bush. The civilian officials at Ishasha told everyone what the police officers had done, and everyone in the pharmaceutical business heard what had happened. When the police officers questioned me I thought to myself, 'This is the way Chika was killed!' 'You are a new face here,' they said. 'People from Bukavu don't use this border. We are going to take you to Goma to see the authorities.' I started shaking, and begged them to let me go. I was arrested and put in a cell.

I sat in the cell thinking, 'I am going to die. They know what happened in Bukavu, that's why they arrested me.' There was a quarantine officer called Buuma at the border post who I knew a bit. He had seen me when I was waiting, and asked the police, 'What happened to Isaac?' 'Who is Isaac?' they said. 'Is that the short fat man?' Buuma asked, 'Why did you arrest him? I know he isn't a bad man.' The senior police officer told him that if I wanted to be released I should pay $5000. I offered $500, because I didn't know why I had been arrested in the first place. I still didn't think I had done anything wrong at the workshop in Kigali. The police officers were insulted with my offer and got angry, and the image of Chika came to me again. I talked to Buuma, and he suggested I offer $2500.

I paid $2500 to the police officer but then the prison guard demanded money to return my shoes and belt, which had been taken off me when I was arrested. I protested I had just paid $2500 but the police officer said I had to sort it out with the guard and could not go until I did. I paid the guard another $20 to get my shoes and belt back.

I had been in the cell for about an hour. When I got out Buuma helped me cross into Uganda. I was shaking and crying. He said, 'Isaac! You're a man. Don't cry! You'll get $2500 again.' I didn't want to tell him what had happened in Bukavu, that I had had to sell my building.

Telling this story reminds me that I was prosperous. I had a commercial building and was renting each shop. If I never worked again, I could make a living from that building. What makes me sad is that when you become an activist you are doing nothing wrong but you can suffer. Really, even today I don't know what I did that made me have to sell that building for $15,000 … It was an icon when it was built! Everybody knew it was 'the Pygmy man's building'. It was the biggest, nicest building in that part of the city. There was a steep path beside it that the public used to get to the market. The path was a mess and I didn't want customers to slip when it rained so I paid for concrete stairs and a wooden handrail to be built. People could not believe that I had used my own money to help the public. No-one does that in Congo. They said that I should be the mayor!

Why was I put into a cell? I didn't insult anyone. They took my money, cheated me. I didn't do anything wrong.

When I finally made it across the border I felt depressed. I thought about all the money I had spent. All the money I had wasted. I caught a bus to Kampala and I found Josephine and the kids at the Exotic Inn. When I told Josephine what had happened at Bunagana we cried together. Nothing had happened to Josephine on her own journey, but she had been anxious and stressed about me. We didn't have mobile phones back then so she didn't know what was happening to me and I didn't know what was happening to her and the kids, but she had taken the bus to Kigali, where she stayed overnight with a Tutsi friend, then continued on to Kampala the next day.

Uganda was part of the alliance with Rwanda and the RCD against the Congolese government, and the secret police were in Kampala, so on the Monday we bought bus tickets to Nairobi. I didn't feel completely safe staying in Uganda. We arrived in Nairobi on 12 January 2001, and on the 15th I went to register with the UNHCR as a refugee.

21

Just a refugee

We rented a one-bedroom flat on the second floor of an apartment block being built in Pangani, a busy neighbourhood of Nairobi. The owner was already renting out the apartments even though the building was still under construction. All my neighbours were Kenyan, although there was a Congolese family and some Ethiopians in the next apartment block. We had fled Congo with few possessions and there was nothing in the flat. It had a kitchen with a sink, and that was it. I had a mattress and bought some Muslim prayer mats, which are cheap, for the children to sleep on, and we all slept in a row on the floor.

I didn't know this when I arrived in Nairobi, but the UNHCR local office was going through big changes. The new manager was called Sergio, and he was from South America. The UNHCR had to deal with refugees from many countries: Congo, Rwanda, Burundi, Sudan, Ethiopia, Eritrea and Somalia. Sergio decided that each nationality had to be represented by one person in its dialogue with the UNHCR because he didn't want different delegations coming to see him all the time. He told each national community to elect a representative, and the day I registered at the UNCHR the Congolese community was organising a vote to elect a leader and a deputy leader.

In Nairobi I immediately met many other Congolese, including many people from Bukavu. Some of them were former customs officials I used to have to bribe when I brought pharmaceuticals into Congo. They were surprised to see me at the UNHCR office, and called me Vieux Isaac, Old Isaac, out of respect. The Congolese who recognised me knew I was a businessman with a good reputation, and knew my two-storey building in Bukavu. Some of them used to visit my pharmacy and others knew I had paid for the stairs beside my building. They asked me to stand for election to be the Congolese community's leader in dealings with UNHCR. Those Congolese who had been there for a long time said, 'He's just arrived! How can he represent us?' The ones who knew me told them, 'No. He can lead us. We know him.' I decided to put my name down to be a candidate.

I was still affected by my experience at the border crossing at Bunagana, so the vote was a good distraction. It was also a competition to win, and I like competition. It is part of my character that I don't like someone else telling me what to do – I prefer to make the decisions myself. Those former customs officers campaigned for me and there were many people from Bukavu at the meeting compared to other areas of Eastern Congo.

I won the vote! I had become the Nairobi Congolese community's official contact with the UNHCR. We had to choose a deputy leader as well, and I said that if we wanted credibility in the eyes of Sergio we should elect a Congolese Tutsi, otherwise he would think we discriminated against Tutsis. One of the unsuccessful candidates for my position was a Tutsi, Etienne, and he was voted in as the deputy.

We went to meet Sergio and were issued with a formal paper with my photograph attached and Sergio's signature at the bottom, saying I was the representative of the Congolese community. In the following days people who had not been at the meeting started to complain. They disapproved of the election, said they did not accept the result and said we should vote again. 'How could someone who has just registered as a refugee become the leader?' they asked. They tried to complain to Sergio but he refused to see them. There were similar problems in the Sudanese, Eritrean and Rwandan communities, and Sergio said whoever had been elected was now the official leader.

I started to meet with the UNHCR when they wanted to discuss matters involving the Congolese community. They were busy because in April, Kofi Annan, the UN Secretary General, visited Nairobi. One of things he did was announce that there would be an investigation into corruption in the UNCHR. There were allegations that UNHCR staff took bribes to resettle refugees or to get refugee children accepted for resettlement as part of someone else's family. Refugees who had paid bribes but did not get resettlement were upset and had complained.

One morning, about 10 am when I had gone to the UNHCR office and Josephine was at home alone with the children, four men from the Criminal Investigations Department of the Kenya police, the CID, came to our flat. I found out later that the RCD regime had provided them with intelligence about me and said I should be arrested.

Those police opened everything. They searched through all our bags, looked in the pockets of our clothing and at documents. They took documents that were written in French back to their office, including the constitution of APDMAC and letters I had from Minority Rights Group with information about the financial support they were giving me to travel to Durban for the UN conference. We had $10,000 in cash but Josephine was wearing this in a sock tied around her waist, under her wrap, and they did not find it. Josephine was scared and she did what everyone in Congo did when harassed by the police: offered them money. The lead investigator refused! 'We did not come here for money,' he said. We were surprised to hear a police officer say that. In Congo the police never, never, never refuse money.

When I talk to Congolese about corruption they say soldiers aren't paid and President Kabila is weak and this is why there is corruption, but they have never seen how things work in other countries. Kenya is known as a very corrupt country, but if I got stopped by the police in Nairobi they would ask for a very small amount of money and then let me go. If you really protested, sometimes they would leave you alone completely. Or, if you gave some money and then went to police headquarters to complain to the police chief that Officer So-and-So had asked for a bribe, the police chief would take action and the police officer would be in trouble with his boss. In Congo, this never happens. In Kenya the police are corrupt a bit, but you cannot *bargain* over bribes the way everyone does openly in Congo.

When I got home from UNHCR Josephine was upset and told me what had happened. The neighbours were also worried and one told me that if it was the CID who came, that meant it was a serious matter. The investigators had left a letter requesting that I go to police headquarters. I did not understand how they had found me or what the problem was. Nairobi is a tough, expensive city and crime is high. I was new there and did not know how anything worked, and I did not have anyone to go to for help.

I knew that I had not killed anyone or committed a crime,

and I also knew there was no way I could run away again as I had ten children to look after. I decided I could not hide and had to go to the police headquarters and speak to the investigators. A Kenyan neighbour encouraged me, saying that if they had asked me to come in for questioning that might mean the matter was not too serious, because if it had been very serious they would have returned to arrest me.

The next day I went to the CID. An investigator was assigned to take my statement, and he asked so many questions. Why had I fled Congo? Why did I think they had refused me permission to go to Durban? What was I doing in Nairobi? What organisations had supported me and APDMAC? He was very different to Congolese policemen. He looked caring and did not threaten or try to intimidate me. I told the investigator about the workshops I had attended in Kigali, Kampala and Bujumbura, and said that the rebel regime's secret police had found out about these and detained me. I told the investigator how they accused me of going to these conferences simply to give a bad name to the RCD. I gave him details of my contacts for the Forest Peoples Programme, Minority Rights Group and Survival International.

He asked me so many questions about being a Pygmy. He said that in Kenya they learn about Pygmies in school, and told me that he had heard we were oppressed and seen as subhuman. He never believed that he would meet or interview a Pygmy. He thought we all lived in far-off forests. 'Yes,' I said, 'that's what Congolese say, that we are just in the forest. They don't want us to say in conferences that we are oppressed.' I think he started to understand what had happened to me. The interview took hours, but when it was over, I felt better.

I returned the following week to sign my statement. I had been curious about why I was picked by the CID from all the Congolese refugees who were in Nairobi at that time, and I asked the investigator. He was straight with me: 'We are not magicians. We received intelligence from Congo that we should investigate why you fled and what you are doing here. That is our job, and that is why we went to your flat. We were just checking if what we were told was true.' I assume the rebels wanted the Kenyan government to deport me back to Congo.

I had had to go to police headquarters several times to finalise my statement and over time I became familiar with some of the investigators because I always had to wait for several hours. I used to chat to them, especially the one who took my statement. The first time I had come in they asked, 'Are you Isaac?' as though they did not believe it. This puzzled me, but an investigator explained that because of the intelligence the police had received they had expected a big man, a rich man, who had fled with a lot of money. They were surprised that the rich and dangerous man they expected was living in a one-bedroom flat with no bed, one mattress on the floor and ten children. The investigator told me that his chief thought the rebel regime in Eastern Congo had lied and exaggerated about me.

The CID dropped my case.

The criticism of me being leader of the Congolese refugee community in those early months in Nairobi never went away. There were many Bembe people from southern South Kivu registered in Nairobi and they said, 'Isaac knows nothing about refugee life! He knows nothing about the UNHCR!' There was a lot of argument. One day Sergio told me he had had too many complaints from the Congolese community and suggested I step down from being leader. He also said that the investigation team sent by the UN's Office of Internal Oversight Services to investigate corruption in UNHCR needed consultants familiar with the Congolese community. I could not really be effective if the Congolese refugee community did not support me, and I also needed a job because surviving was very hard. We were living on the $10,000 I had brought to Nairobi and we had no other source of income. I decided to resign and see if I could get a job as a consultant on the investigation.

I went to see the UN's chief investigator on the case, Frank Montil. Frank was a serious man. He wore dark glasses and dressed in a khaki jacket with pockets on the chest. Frank started speaking English to me but my English wasn't very good then. Frank is Australian, but his mother was French and his French language is very good, so from that moment on we spoke in French. He started explaining what he was investigating and telling me how he needed certain people in the community contacted – those who had paid bribes, and those whose money was taken but nothing was done – and the kinds of questions that needed to be asked. He asked if I knew how to find certain addresses in different parts of Nairobi, and then asked how many languages I spoke. I told him French, Swahili, Kinyarwanda, Kirundi and a few others. This was essential for the job because the refugees, the witnesses, spoke these languages. Many of them had not been to school so did not speak French and maybe not even Swahili. I told Frank I could do the job and I was hired as a consultant on the investigation. Because I could not speak English very well, Frank let me write my reports in French.

Frank answered to Barbara, who was based in New York. She was also an investigator. Barbara was talkative and joked a bit – Frank never joked – but she always focused on the job I was doing. She couldn't believe I had ten children at 39, and often asked about them.

Frank hired two other Congolese for the small team that was to work with refugees from Central Africa. One was called Jean and I forget the other one, but he had been a general manager of a local government in Congo. They spoke many languages as well. There were other teams for the other refugee groups, such as Sudanese, Eritrean and Somali. On our third day at work a problem arose. Frank asked me, Jean and the other man to each do a project budget for the people we were to interview, who were in different parts of Nairobi. We did our budgets, working out transport costs and meal allowances. This was the money we needed to do the job, on top of our salaries. Our budgets were very different. Mine was 3000 Kenyan shillings (about $40), Jean's was 15,000 shillings and the other man's was 25,000 shillings. Frank showed the budgets to some Kenyan colleagues to check if the prices were right and I saw him become cranky, muttering about what was in the budgets. Frank came back to us and the third man's budget was immediately refused and he was told to leave, but Jean and I were hired. Jean asked me how much I had put down, and when I told him 3000 shillings he said, 'Why did you put that? We should have budgeted the same amount and profited from the job, but you destroyed it!' Actually, I was already making a profit, although I didn't tell Jean that. I knew I could get cabbage and *ugali* for about 25 cents but I had budgeted 65 cents per meal, hoping to get an extra 40 cents per meal to take home.

I met the first person I was supposed to interview and he gave me his story about how he had offered his bribe to the UNHCR staff member. I then brought the statement back to Frank. When Frank thought a witness had sensitive things to say I had to bring the witness to Frank for a second interview. Frank only wanted to see those people with something serious to say. At the end of the month I was paid 16,000 shillings as my salary, about $210. I was very excited when I got my first salary. I bought a cardigan for Josephine, some shoes for the kids and we all went to the market to buy a nice fish for dinner.

So I started working like that. Eventually Frank gave me permission to do interviews with refugees from other countries as well, not just Central Africa. He was concerned to get good evidence from as many witnesses as possible. At the end of my second month my probationary period was over and I got a contract. There was a lot of work because it could take several weeks to finish a statement. I had to do a budget for each potential witness, then locate the person, convince them to cooperate, question them, write up the statement, show it to Frank, and bring the person to Frank for a second interview if he thought it worthwhile. Sometimes I might have to visit the person three or four times. Later on, when the case went through the courts, I also accompanied each of my witnesses.

There were some witnesses who admitted that they gave bribes, but did not want to complain. They accepted that they had lost their money. Some told me they had hunted the UNHCR officials and begged them to take their bribes. The officials took the money but said there was no guarantee that they would get resettlement, but that they would try to help. One Ethiopian man who had given money to an official said the official had been honest with him because he hadn't promised anything. 'Keep it anyway, just in case,' he told the official. The Ethiopian man said because he had forced the official to take the money he was not going to take him to court. The bribe-payers who refused to complain blamed the other bribe-payers for disclosing their secrets. The refugees who gave big amounts of money could not just leave the matter, however. They had no hope for resettlement because two or three years had passed and they had given all the money they had to someone in UNHCR. They hoped that by going to court they could at least get back their money.

Frank gave me a desk and a computer in the UN office. I wrote my reports very slowly because I was not good at typing. The head of the area I was working in was a man called Njoroge, a Kenyan. He was jealous because he could not read French. 'I'm the boss and I can't read this!' he protested. I continued working on the investigation but I started to worry about my safety. Kenyan UN staff were not happy with the investigation because some of them knew the people who had taken bribes. Some of their colleagues had already been fired – they had lost good jobs, well-paying jobs, and faced court. Njoroge kept saying, 'This will make Kenya look bad!'

I told Frank that I felt my security was at risk because of my job. I also felt vulnerable because of the search of our flat by the Kenyan CID. I said that the job might look easy, but that if he looked deeper he would see that it was risky. In Nairobi you can pay someone $200 to kill a person. I asked Frank if he could find me different accommodation, in a safer neighbourhood, and he arranged for my family to stay at the YMCA hotel. Later, when I accompanied my witnesses to court, those former UNHCR officials on trial looked at me as a big enemy. I remember one official who denied ever knowing the man, my witness, who had given him a bribe. When court was over we went outside and that official was having a smoke. He had a cigarette between his teeth and his face was full of anger towards me.

I thought the Kenyans at the UN and in the courts were trying hard to protect the Kenyans who had taken bribes, but they didn't care about the Europeans working for UNCHR who had been corrupt. About sixty or seventy people in the UNHCR and an NGO had taken money from refugees, who paid up to $5000 for their applications to be processed. Nine people were eventually arrested and charged by the Kenyan police.

My other big problem in Nairobi was that I was disadvantaged with my limited English skills. Swahili is a national language in Kenya so I had no problems speaking with people on the street or in offices, but this did not give me much motivation to learn English. The Ethiopians and Somalis did not speak Swahili at all, so they put all their effort into learning English and learnt it faster than I did. But in the UNHCR office everything was written in English and I had problems understanding documents. Everything was also on a computer and I did not know much about them either. The fact that Njoroge knew more English than me and that English is the top language of the UN motivated me to learn English and to write reports in English. I enrolled in private English classes and in a computer course. I slowly gained confidence and could better understand the content of documents at work with the help of a dictionary.

I answered directly to Frank on the investigation but I had to sit in the same office as Njoroge, who did not tolerate me. He was upset because he thought Frank should have employed a Kenyan but had instead chosen me – a Congolese who was 'just a refugee'. Njoroge was against everything I did and spoke badly about Frank hiring me. 'I don't understand how a refugee could have this job, especially when there are Kenyans who need jobs!' he used to say. Other staff supported him and said refugees should not have been employed on an investigation. They said I was being given authority over former UNHCR officers, who were the ones being investigated.

Njoroge asked to see my reports, but I didn't show them to him and this made him unhappy. Several times I came into the office and found that he had accessed the reports on my computer. Njoroge's deputy, a nice Kenyan lady, told me that Njoroge had taken them to someone else who spoke French to find out what I was writing. 'You are writing a lot of lies!' Njoroge told me. It was a difficult situation. I told Frank what had happened and he told me to stop using the UN computers to email my reports. I had to save them onto a floppy disk, erase everything from the work computer, then go to a cyber café and email the reports from there. I kept working like this, but there was pressure on me whenever I went into the office.

Despite the problems at work, it was a happy life. I was well paid, the job was interesting and I felt useful. Frank told me how much he appreciated my reports because they were accurate and full of evidence. Not even on one occasion did Frank change anything I had written in my reports. When Frank first introduced me to Barbara, in a very enthusiastic way she said, 'Oh, Frank has spoken to me about you!' I felt very respected.

My life was not of a very high standard but it was also not very poor. I was getting my salary and I did not have to pay for accommodation because the UN was paying for that. I also got money for meals during the days when I was interviewing witnesses, and I got free transport with the UN bus that picked up staff from around Nairobi and took them to work. I could save money, and this allowed me to pay for private schools for my kids.

I was determined to send Wetekay, my eldest son, to a good school. I told myself that I didn't want to save anything, I just wanted to invest in my kids. I enrolled Wetekay in a private boys' high school. He was studying with the son of the Congolese Ambassador to Kenya, as well as the sons of Kenyan politicians and rich Indians. My daughter Zawadi is also intelligent. She was always first, second or third in her class. I enrolled her in a private high school as well. It was expensive but not as much as Wetekay's school. Bikulo and Luko'o also went to private schools, but Abner and Abishay went to public schools. Jamaa and Deborah were now too old for school, and Boaz and Jamaa's son Jonathan, were all too young. I was using three-quarters of my income on sending my kids to school, thinking about an education that could help them and their future.

Josephine and the kids were happy in Nairobi. Wetekay felt proud that he was going to a good school. He thought he was high class. The others had started to learn English in school. In Congo people feel proud if they can speak English, so the children were happy to be learning this in school. Josephine looked after the home, with help from Jamaa and Deborah.

But I had ten children in Nairobi, including my grandson Jonathan. Raising ten kids is totally different to raising two or three. Ten children means ten different personalities, ten different behaviours. There is rivalry amongst them to get the best school results. Sometimes if they got good results we could not reward them by buying something because our income was too limited. When it comes to feeding a family, someone with two or three kids can buy a couple of loaves of bread and that's enough. We eventually had fourteen people in our household in Nairobi after we had another baby and my nephew Akili came to live with us from Congo. Sometimes, having bought two loaves of bread for dinner, by dinner time some of the bread has already been eaten. It was impossible to find which child stole the bread. That was a big challenge for us.

It was in Nairobi that we had our last child, Montil. The motivation of naming Montil was to give recognition to Frank Montil, the UN investigator, for what he had done for me: for giving me a job and treating me with respect. Frank is a person who has marked my life and the best way I could show my gratitude was to give my son his name. If someone had helped me in Congo we would bring a nice rooster for them. This is the BaTembo custom for showing gratitude. But Frank did not need a rooster, so we named our son after him instead.

We stopped having more children after Montil because of those Kenyans, who do not like lots of children. Once when Josephine went to hospital they said, 'Why do you have so many kids? Your husband wants to kill you!' Josephine had been diagnosed with diabetes and the doctors said this could be dangerous for another pregnancy. They pressured her to have a tubal ligation so she could not have more children. This was against my wishes but it happened anyway. Josephine's sister has fourteen children, so I would have been happy for Josephine to have children until she got to menopause, so another three or four kids. But Josephine was happy with the tubal ligation. Since she had been in Nairobi she had started to see things differently because of the influence of the Kenyans, who think like white people.

22

Meeting the light

In January 2003 my work on the investigation into UNHCR corruption came to an end. Njoroge did something or said something to someone, I am not quite sure what, and I lost my job and could not get any more contracts with the UN. Frank had been told that he had to employ Kenyans on the investigation. 'Njoroge has won,' he told me.

Everything changed. I had to leave the YMCA hotel and start paying rent. We went to live in Eastleigh, the business area for Somalis, and I rented a two-bedroom apartment. Josephine and I had one bedroom, the girls had the other, and all the boys slept in the living room. I had not saved any money from my UN salary because I was spending most of it educating my children, but we still had about five or six thousand dollars left from selling the building in Bukavu and we used this to live. The UNHCR told me to go to a refugee camp but I didn't want to go. I had seen refugee camps full of tents in Congo, and in Kenya the camps were in the desert, far from Nairobi. I preferred to keep renting the small apartment in Eastleigh.

I asked Frank if he knew of any jobs and he said there might be work for the UN in Kinshasa, but I was afraid of returning to Congo, even if it was to the government-held side. In 2002 there had been a peace agreement between all the countries fighting in Congo, but foreign troops had not yet left the east. Josephine liked the idea of going back, but I told her that once the job in Kinshasa finished we would be stuck there, unable to return to Bukavu because of the RCD. Frank asked me where I would like to go and I said, 'America!' He told me, 'You only like America because you have never been there. There is little support for migrants in America and the first years will not be good.' He said countries like Australia offer more support, so then I thought, 'Australia!' That same month, January, I put in an application to the Australian Embassy for resettlement.

When I was in Congo I had no idea about Australia. In school we learnt there was 'Oceania' and that Australia was part of it, and that was it. After I had put in my application, I started to read about Australia on the internet. When I saw a map I thought it was just a big desert, and this put a question mark in my head. Then, on KBC TV, we saw an advertisement for a documentary about Australia that they were going to show the following Sunday. All week we were really looking forward to that Sunday, to know what Australia was like. The documentary showed clear rivers with a lot of crabs like we had back in the Kasachi Forest! Australia looked exactly like the forest from back home. I started to think about how I could do *kukiya* – create channels to divert the creek – to catch fish and crabs. I thought we could go to the place in the documentary and catch crabs for free and put traps in the river to catch fish. We wondered how we could make fish traps – whether there were the same vines in the forest – but Josephine said the people living near the river would know how to make traps. I think the documentary was probably about northern Queensland.

While we were waiting to hear back from the Australian Embassy we lived on Josephine's income. She had started selling clothes, helped by Jamaa and Deborah. They sold African wraps used as skirts by women, to earn some money. Congolese have the highest reputation in Africa for dressing well – all the best-dressed people in Nairobi are Congolese – so other Africans think it is natural that Congolese will sell fashionable clothes. Josephine and a group of other Congolese women would go into the city and try to get past watchmen to enter multistorey buildings with office and government workers. Because the watchmen would never let them in directly, what the women did instead was wait by the entrance or in the car park and when a government minister or other senior person came out they would approach him and say they had beautiful wraps for his wife. The man would tell the watchman to let Josephine into the building and then once inside, she would visit other office workers. The ladies would look at everything and buy something, or Josephine would get an IOU and come back several days later to collect the money. The Kenyan customers felt sorry for Josephine and the other refugee ladies so they would let them visit their offices. In Congo this would be impossible. First, you cannot approach a minister. Second, if you are a foreigner they would first ask to see your licence to sell something. If you had no licence then you could not sell anything, so the police would just steal all the merchandise. In Congo we would never see good people like those Kenyans! Despite their poverty, they were good and kind and felt sorry for refugees.

I had to find work and decided to look for a teaching job in one of the schools for refugees in Nairobi's townships. I went to see a school principal I knew to ask if he had any jobs available, although it turned out there were none. On the bus on the way there, I noticed one of the investigators, a low-ranking officer, I had dealt with after the CID raided our flat when we first arrived in Nairobi. He also recognised me and we greeted each other and sat together. I had always been curious as to how the CID had come to know about my existence in Nairobi, why they picked me from all the Congolese refugees in the city at that time, so I finally asked. He explained that there was a Congolese man in Nairobi who spied on Congolese expatriates for the rebel regime, and that this man had told the CID about me. The investigator told me that even his boss felt sorry for me and thought the police had wasted their time.

I had some money so when we got off the bus together I invited him to have some grilled kebabs and beer with me. The investigator told me that the Congolese spy lived close by to where we were, but that I had to be very, very careful if I saw him and should not tell anyone that the investigator had given me the information. This spy was a dangerous man, but I wanted to locate and know this man so I could protect myself against him.

There were other Congolese refugees around and I asked them if they knew him. They said, 'Yes, we know him. He is a Tutsi from Goma.' One asked why I wanted to know, but I remembered what the policeman had said and did not explain. Together with another Congolese who I knew a bit, I wandered past this man's house. As it turned out the other Congolese knew the spy, and the spy's door was open so we went inside and greeted him.

The spy did not look scary. He was of medium build and had a long nose. He fixed a lot of attention on me, asking where I was from and where I lived in Bukavu, but I was nervous and he noticed. Suddenly his demeanour changed. He became still and very alert and uneasy. I think at that instant he realised who I was and sensed that I knew what he had done to me. Oh, he wasn't expecting me to visit! And he certainly did not understand how I could come to be in his house! We didn't stay long and afterwards I left that neighbourhood quickly.

The Australian Embassy eventually telephoned to arrange an interview about my application for resettlement. I always wonder if Frank said something to them about the risks I faced on the UNHCR investigation, and if this helped me get an interview. Even though I was no longer working on the investigation the pressure on me from UNHCR staff had not stopped, for there were rumours circulating – and I think these had reached the Australian Embassy – that I had declared ten children as belonging to me when other people had actually bribed me to take their children to Australia. The rumours were that my son, Wetekay, was my eldest child and that Jamaa, Deborah and Zawadi were the daughters of other people. People said that Frank had been working with a liar – me – and that liars were investigating UNHCR staff accused of taking bribes from refugees, when I had also taken bribes to pretend that other people's children were mine. Part of the rumour was that it was impossible for me to have become a grandfather at 39. In fact, this had happened because my eldest daughter, Jamaa, had a child from when she became pregnant at seventeen in Congo. Kenyans just didn't believe that someone could have ten children and be a grandfather so young. Congolese have no trouble believing this.

The embassy sent the whole family to have DNA tests, although we didn't know they were going to do this. They just said we were having medical tests. They took everyone's blood and after a few days we went for a second test at the same place. A laboratory technician told me the tests showed that all the kids belonged to me, but the embassy needed a second test so it could compare results. The technician told me: 'If we do the second test here they will think you bribed us to change the results, because refugees always try to bribe.' Because of all the rumours I had to get a second test at a different place, and I was sent to Nairobi Private Hospital. At the hospital they said they only needed to test Josephine, me and the three girls, and they found our DNA matched.

The tests were done to catch me out but instead they gave me confidence in Josephine and my children. They knew 100 per cent that I was their dad. I was reminded of my own family, because we were never sure if our father was really our father. The life I was living with Josephine was totally different to that of my parents. I never suspected Josephine of being with someone else. I felt proud I had no *enfants douteux*, doubtful children. I knew they were all mine.

In May 2003 I got the news that we had been accepted for resettlement. We were going to Sydney! We were all so happy! The whole family became very interested in Australia and whenever I went to the cyber café I googled life in Sydney. All the pictures were very attractive. I went through the statistics for poverty and found that there was no poverty compared to Africa. I knew that everyone could find something to eat, and that it was hard to find a normal person with nowhere to live because the government provided housing for unemployed people. I also researched the unemployment rate and saw that it was low, and I read about the high lifestyle in Australia – higher than many European countries. Josephine and the kids were also excited. We had a two-bedroom apartment with fourteen people and felt very confined. We started to think about how we could live in a big house. We bought nice shoes and clothing, and bags to carry our things.

The medical tests had revealed one problem. Jonathan, my grandson, was found to have hepatitis B. The embassy said that he could not travel with this sickness and that he needed to be treated first. When he was better he could follow us, and this is what happened. Jamaa stayed with him while he received treatment and arrived in Australia six months after us.

The day before we left I hired a minibus to carry us and our bags to a house run by GOAL, an Irish NGO, for refugees in transit. The next morning at 6 am we were taken to Jomo Kenyatta International Airport. I had been on a plane before for business trips but this was the first time Josephine and the kids had entered a plane. I told them it was just like being on the ferry from Bukavu to Goma when there were no waves – stable. Everybody was excited. We flew with Kenya Airways to Johannesburg in South Africa. When we left the plane we saw a man holding a sign saying 'Bacirongo family'. He was from the International Organization for Migration and bought us chicken and chips while we waited for the flight to Australia. In Nairobi all the black people spoke Swahili, but in Johannesburg they all spoke English. We started to practise our English on them. The Qantas flight to Sydney was on a very big plane with three rows of seats stretching all the way down to the back. It was like being on a big ship. When we saw the crew and passengers we said, 'They are the people we are going to live with!' They were 99 per cent white. Only our family and two or three Sudanese sitting far away were black.

I wasn't thinking about Congo at all when the plane took off. To me, it was Gehenna from the Jewish Bible – the hell where people suffer day and night. I just had bad memories about that place. Everything was positive, positive, positive about where I was going.

When we left Johannesburg it was night. Then we met the light, the sun. I looked out of the window at the ocean and saw that it was very huge. On the route map on the TV screen I eventually saw that we had entered Australia. I looked down and saw lakes and thought there must be a lot of fish in this country. I like fish, and seeing those lakes gave me a guarantee that we would be having a lot of fish when we were settled. I could see vegetation and farms, and something that I thought were grapes growing in straight lines. I loved the arrangement of the farms! I could see that one farm was next to another, and that each had clear limits.

I thought it was paradise.

23

Finding real life

When we first arrived in Sydney we could have burst with joy. My chest was full of happiness. The government gave us about $1800 each fortnight to survive. Free money. It was a miracle! This is the kind of miracle I can believe in, unlike witchcraft or the Holy Spirit. There was also an abundance of food and we didn't need to think too much about whether we could afford it. I used to buy an entire lamb, or a whole leg of cow, from the butcher. Even when I had a good life in Congo I never bought a whole leg of cow, but in Australia I could do it. And there was a diversity of foods. We had lamb, cow and chicken in the fridge, and fish. We also had fruits and processed foods, and could afford to drink milk every morning, so we put milk and sugar in our tea instead of drinking it black with no sugar. After a few months we all put on weight.

The government put us in short-term accommodation for one month, then we had to find a place to rent. Finding a place big enough for us all was difficult, but eventually we found a five-bedroom, double-storey fibro house in the City of Fairfield in Western Sydney.

The people around Fairfield did not have money, they were just workers, although some are now demolishing their old houses and building new double-storey ones. The people were migrants and refugees, mostly Arabs, from Iraq, and Asian, especially Vietnamese, Cambodian and Chinese. There were a few Eastern Europeans as well. There was no English spoken in homes –

everyone was speaking their own language. I had a neighbour who said, 'Me, Romania! Me, Romania!' and he brought a case of beer to share but we couldn't talk to each other. Coming from Africa, I thought everyone was rich because in Africa we define 'rich' as having three meals a day, a house and a car. Now I know the difference between rich and poor, but at that time, according to my definition, everyone was rich.

The image of Sydney I had seen in Nairobi on the internet was very different to what I experienced in Fairfield. On the internet there was only the Harbour Bridge, Sydney Tower and beaches, but I found that the beach was not in Fairfield. A Polish man took us into the city to show us how Sydney looked at night. He bought us some beer and we walked around excitedly until 2 am. It was not like Fairfield. No, no, no, no, no! It's a long way from Fairfield. But Fairfield had nice streets and we had two shopping malls close to us. What impressed me was that everyone, poor or rich, was shopping there. In Nairobi, shopping malls like that are only for rich people. We had just arrived but we were also shopping there.

Many things increased our joy of living. The environment in Fairfield was so clean – the streets were clean! – and there was no dust like in Congo in the dry season. There were twelve of us in our new house: Josephine and me, and the children – Deborah, who was nineteen; Zawadi, seventeen; Wetekay, sixteen; my nephew, Akili, who was fifteen; Abner, thirteen; Abishay, twelve; Bikulo, ten; Luko'o, eight; Boaz, four; and Montil, two. Josephine and I had our own bedroom and there were two or three children in each of the other bedrooms, so in Australia we started to breathe again. Josephine and I attended English language classes and these were free, provided by the government. Josephine even got free childcare for Boaz and Montil when she went to class. Six months after we arrived, our eldest daughter Jamaa and her son, Jonathan, came and moved into a unit in a different suburb, so the whole family was in Sydney.

Deborah, Zawadi, Wetekay, Akili, Abner, Abishay, Bikulo and Luko'o enrolled in local schools. The kids had some English because they had learnt it in school in Nairobi, and they could talk directly to the teachers. Their English was better than the kids from Afghanistan or Iran, or the kids from refugee camps in Tanzania where children only learnt Swahili. Because the children spoke English, this gave them pride and confidence at school. To be a foreigner in the schools they attended was also normal because Fairfield is full of immigrants, so they did not feel too different from the other kids.

But we all wanted to become Australian. This reminds me of one of our Pygmy proverbs, '*Ukaya erabulya susi, nau wanalya kusi*': 'If you go where the people eat flies, you should also eat flies.' It is the KiTembo way of saying, 'When in Rome, do as the Romans do'. We wanted to be like Australians.

During our first year in Australia the kids were never a problem because, at the ages they were then, they are only a problem if they do not have enough to eat. If they have full stomachs, they can watch television or play in the park and they are happy. I thought the problems people in Australia have about their kids – this worrying all the time – was just in their minds. A friend of mine had his first child at 51. I asked if he planned to have a second and he said, 'No more!' I was surprised, because having one child is not a burden. He and his wife are comfortable and materially they have no problem providing for that one child. Sometimes we meet someone with three dogs, but only one or two children. When children are born at first you do everything for them; when they are about three they can go to the toilet alone; when they are five you take them to school; when they are seven they start doing many things for themselves and help at home, such as clearing the dishes from the table. Kids grow up and become independent. But with a dog, after four, five or ten years you will still be taking out its shit. Dogs remain dependent on you until they die. This idea that children are a burden, we don't share that thinking.

Some things about Australia surprised me. When I went to the countryside I saw that even there all the houses have electricity and access to roads. I liked this a lot. In the countryside there is also a lot of meat. Once I drove to Adelaide with four of the kids and we returned through the outback. My GPS stopped working and somehow we got lost. We drove for hundreds of kilometres without seeing another person, but we suddenly saw goats alongside the road. We jumped out hoping to catch one of the goats to eat. We thought we could put it in the car and take it home to Sydney, but the goats all ran away. It reminded me of antelope hunting in Congo. In Australia there is meat just running around. All those kangaroos are meat!

I also immediately liked that the Australian authorities were approachable. They were not terrifying or intimidating people like in Congo. I was not even scared of the police and my interaction with them has never been too bad.

The free newspapers surprised me – the local ones sent to everyone's home. I wondered how much it cost to write this newspaper and distribute it for free. What was bizarre was that on the back page of those newspapers there were notices from prostitutes, advertising themselves. In Fairfield there was a house where prostitutes stayed, where you could meet them and enjoy sex with them. That house was just there! In Nairobi, or Congo or Kampala there are prostitutes, but they are not organised like here and the government would ban such houses.

I was also surprised that women here showed their bodies. African women normally cover their body, especially their thighs and breasts, although in the forest growing up it was totally different. In the forest both men and women had uncovered torsos. Bantus used to give us cloth to cover ourselves. They thought we dressed like that because of poverty and being uncivilised, but it was because clothes in the forest catch on branches and slow you down. In Australia, it is not because of poverty that women show their bodies: they think it is fashionable.

A few months after we arrived I started volunteering for the Fairfield Migrant Resource Centre. I helped other refugees get access to government services, showed them how to use public transport and explained things about Australian culture. For example, the way women are viewed in Africa and in Muslim cultures is different from the way women are viewed in Australia. I explained to newly arrived families that here, women share power in the family. There is equality. I told them that there are no separate jobs for men and women, even domestic jobs. Both men and women do these jobs in Australia. Some men would tell me, 'That's impossible!' They would take the Christian viewpoint that men are the head of the household and that God made men dominant, and women should be submissive. Most refugee men found that when they arrived here they lost their power as family head. This did not happen to me, because since I married Josephine we shared power in our house. We've never had 'my' money and 'her' money. Josephine is the caretaker of my money and if she loses it, well, it's her problem too. This was the key to my success back home, because I married her with zero and started my business with some money from her mum.

There is no integration into society if you are not doing something with others, especially if you are not working, so I was very motivated to find paid work and not just volunteer. Eventually I got a job with a non-profit organisation that settled refugees in Sydney for the government. It was casual work, not permanent, but the money was better than nothing and I liked it very much. It was similar to the work I did in Nairobi, where I had to meet lots of refugees. I liked helping them settle and I met people from different countries. Working made me feel like the country was welcoming me and I was serving the country. I felt like I had found real life, and it was a good feeling.

I also started to get to know Australians. A year after we arrived I made a close Aboriginal friend called Letty Scott, who was originally from Alice Springs. She first met Josephine, who told her that we were also indigenous. Letty had no idea about Pygmies, had never heard of them! Letty was a Jehovah's Witness and she invited us to her place for coffee and to a Jehovah's Witness meeting. We used to visit each other's homes for dinner. We talked about slavery in Congo, about how Arabs went there to kidnap black people – although Pygmies stayed in the forest and were hard to catch. We also talked about what is common to Aborigines and Pygmies. Letty told me about white Australians and the way they treated her. She said that even if you go to the same church they still look down on you and they do not accept that you have the same abilities. I told her that being a Pygmy is a curse, and that Aborigines in Australia are treated better than Pygmies in Congo. We made a plan to go with Letty to Alice Springs to see her family, but in 2009 she died. I wish she could come back to me. Letty inspired me a lot in regard to enduring oppressive life, and I think Pygmies should follow the Aboriginals' way in Australia.

Once at Petersham train station I was with a friend and an Aboriginal man greeted us. He could see we were black and I thought from the way he looked that he was Aboriginal. He asked, 'Where are you from, brother?' and we said, 'Africa'. He was a lawyer. Another time, at Central station, I met an Aboriginal lady. She was tipsy and talkative, and was coming home from work. She was a nurse. She asked where I was from and told me, 'You're welcome here! Aboriginal people are nice people! We accept other people sharing our land. I don't think other people are hospitable like we are.' I agreed with her.

I was curious to find that mixed-race Aborigines are proud of being Aboriginal. I think it is because the Australian government recognises that the land officially belonged to Aboriginal people before white people came, so the Aboriginal people have some rights and some advantages, such as specific jobs for Aboriginal people. In Congo, especially in Bunyakiri, they know Pygmies are the traditional owners of the land but all the offspring of the mixed Pygmy–Bantu people try to stay on the Bantu side and ignore the Pygmy side, and the government does not have any jobs especially for Pygmies.

After eight months the owner of the house we were renting said he wanted to knock it down and build a new house and he gave us two months' notice to move out. The house had a tiled roof, it was clean and the toilet was working okay, and I could not understand why they wanted to knock down a house that had nothing wrong with it. Moving was a big hassle. It was not easy to find another five-bedroom house. I could only find two-bedroom apartments that we could afford, but they were too small for twelve people and we did not want to live like we had in Nairobi. After two months I hadn't found another place, then three months, then four, then five. Finally I found a four-bedroom house, although the owner had put a bathroom into the garage to make it into another bedroom so there were five bedrooms altogether. The house was good enough for us and we were happy there, but the children had to take the train to school, whereas before they could just walk. We didn't want to change their school as they were settled and it was the middle of the school year.

We started to have many headaches with the children, and just feeding all the kids was a big challenge for us. Eight of our children were going to school so we had eight kids to get up and get ready in the morning. We told the eldest ones to take the youngest ones to primary school on the train, then get back on the train and continue on to high school, but sometimes the eldest ones would just leave and go straight to school and we would have to take the young ones. Other mornings the kids didn't want to wake up at all.

For breakfast we gave the children bread, eggs and tea, but when boys are fourteen or fifteen they can eat a lot. One of them can eat a whole loaf of bread and eight eggs just by himself. Our family used to eat about three dozen eggs and eight loaves of bread a day. We told the kids they would get sick from eating too many eggs, but they never got sick, or fat. We had to shop at the supermarket once or twice a week and the staff there became very friendly with us.

After six months at our new house the owner told us he wanted to sell it, and gave us two months' notice to leave. I felt really unbalanced by having to change house again and the pressure upset me. The problem was not that I was renting, because I had rented in Nairobi even though I had owned houses in Congo. The problem was that I wanted stable conditions and I would have rented a place if I knew I could get it for at least three years. My kids also needed stability. They needed to continue at the same school, and not have to change.

I told myself I had to find my own house, but how could I afford it? I needed to get a mortgage, but to get this I needed a permanent job and to have worked there for two years. At that time I was still working on-call as a case worker for refugee settlement, and my daughter, Deborah, who had trained to be a nursing assistant after leaving high school, had also been working for about one year at a nursing home. I told myself that I had to find a mortgage, but all the mortgage brokers I went to told me I did not meet the criteria. I then heard about a Vietnamese mortgage broker in Cabramatta, called Simon. We visited his office and he started to evaluate our assets and asked us to bring in my and Deborah's payslips. Simon told us that if we had 5 per cent of the price as a deposit, and money for the lawyers to prepare the papers, he should be able to find us a loan based on our combined incomes. All the banks refused, but Simon eventually found a bank willing to lend us money.

I was criticised in the African community, especially by Congolese, because I wanted to buy a house. They told me that I was materialistic and said, 'Many Australians rent. Even people born here can't afford to have a house.' They thought I wanted to show off that I had a house, when I could not really afford it.

While we were looking for a mortgage we were also looking for a house to buy, and we found one nearby in Canley Vale. It was a one-year-old two-storey house, made of white brick with a red tile roof. It had five bedrooms, three bathrooms, four toilets, a double garage, a large kitchen, a big dining room and two storerooms. I liked it because it was located against the backyards of the neighbouring houses. Our children made a lot of noise and sometimes they put the radio up loud, but this house had no other houses very close. The yard also had room for six cars, so I thought that when the kids started to buy cars they could all park inside. There was also a place where I could put a garden and grow beans, bananas, chillies and cassava leaves. I like fresh-from-the-garden food – something I can take from the garden, cook and eat, not something they call fresh that is taken from the garden a week ago and put in the freezer – so having room for a garden was important for me. The house cost $485,000. Deborah and my combined savings covered the 5 per cent deposit, and in February 2006 we took possession.

Something happened to Simon, though. I don't know how the system works, but there was an investigation into mortgage brokers. Some buyers were unable to pay their mortgage, and how these people got their mortgages was investigated, and it was Simon. He had found mortgages for many people who did not meet the criteria. The banks took back the homes of many of his clients and sold them. Simon's mortgage broker licence was also taken back. I was lucky because I got a mortgage. I never would have got one if it wasn't for Simon.

That same year, 2006, I brought Mama to Australia through the government's family migration scheme. Josephine told me to buy her a house in Bukavu to keep her safe, but I would still have to feed her and somehow look after her if she was there. Here, if she gets sick, there is health care. Mama came here through Kampala and it amazed her. She had never been in such a big city. When I spoke to her on the phone she said, 'Thank you, my son. You have brought me to white people's country!' I told her she was still in Africa. I also told her that in Australia people wear shoes and sent her money to buy some. Mama put shoes on for the first time in Kampala and had to learn how to walk in them. She bought a pair of black and white men's sneakers because she didn't know that there were different shoes for men and women.

I brought Mama here because it was an obligation – I had heard that she had suffered badly at the hands of Interahamwe militias operating in Congo. Mama, however, believes I brought her to Australia because the witchcraft from her old witchdoctor finally destroyed Josephine's power over me. When Mama arrived she exclaimed in Swahili, '*Miti shamba ina nguvu njo inatuma mina fika Australia!*': 'Witchcraft is powerful, it has enabled me to arrive in Australia!'

Having Mama here has created tension. Because of all of the attempts by Mama to have Josephine killed, Josephine had become very cautious and I saw that Josephine was right to be scared. You could say Josephine is reluctant to have anything to do with Mama and my family. In Sydney we have a very big house and we could build a small flat in the backyard for Mama, but Mama doesn't live with us. Josephine said, 'No way. It is me or her.' And even now, Mama wants me to divorce Josephine and marry another woman.

They see each other at different gatherings and Mama visits our house very occasionally, but the situation is difficult for me.

Really, Mama has a strong character. She is a tough woman – very, very tough. Tough to live with. She is also still physically strong with the same desires she had when she first married Papa, even though she is about eighty. But she has her own life and I have to accept that she can do whatever she wants. We argue about our beliefs. I told her that all the things people believe in the forest are false. 'You know how you used to believe that underground there was a big animal and when it shook itself it caused erosion in the forest?' I said. 'This animal does not exist. Erosion is caused by heavy rain.' 'No,' said Mama. 'I don't believe what you are saying. You are talking like white people! This animal lives in the forest and no-one has seen it. You just say this because you live in Australia, but if you went back to the forest you should believe in these things.'

Africans in Australia, like Mama, hold on to their beliefs. They just mix what they know from home with their life here, and families back home contribute to this. For example, one weekend in Sydney I visited the home of a middle-aged Congolese woman who had died suddenly. I went there with my family to mourn her. The woman had never married and for the past ten years she had lived with another woman, also Congolese. Neither of them had any children. It is strange for two Congolese women to live together like this. The family back in Congo of the woman who died contacted a leader in the Congolese community in Australia and asked him to find out if the other woman was a witch and had killed their daughter. For them her death was unusual and they could not understand it, so they commissioned the community leader to investigate, to follow the history of the two women living together, to see if they had been quarrelling or having arguments that might have led one to want the other dead.

African churches here also do not help people to move away from their traditional mentality. A few years ago a pastor from Burundi came to Sydney and spoke to African church congregations. He said that he had died for a week: his body had decomposed and he had gone to Heaven, drank wine, eaten chapatis and seen Jesus, but he had then come back to life because his family had prayed for him. When they heard this, everyone in the congregation clapped and raised their hands, and called out 'Ohhh' about the power of the Lord. This Burundian man wanted us to believe that the fact his body was whole and healthy was evidence that he had once been dead. What a lie! Neil Armstrong went to the moon, took photos and brought them back to Earth. *That* is evidence! Even if people here do not agree with what churches say, or with traditional beliefs, they go along with it so they will be accepted by the community. But I do not care about this kind of acceptance.

When I first came to Australia APDMAC wanted me to be a focal point for them, to help get them support. I still have contact with APDMAC and friends and family in Congo, through telephone and email, and I'm always looking to see if there are business opportunities for me there, but when I first came I was more connected to Congo.

A lot of people are suffering back home and there is nothing I can do about it. In the north-east of Congo, a rebel militia went into the Ituri Forest to hunt Pygmies because they thought they could get magic powers from them. One of my aunts was also killed by rebel forces. They found out she was a Pygmy and wanted to learn about Pygmy magic because they thought it would help them in the forest. She told them she knew nothing, so they buried her alive. Sinafasi, one of the founders of APDMAC, went to the United Nations in New York to petition to include cannibalism as a crime against humanity, because other militias were eating Pygmies. The militias thought this would help them in the forest.

I get other bad news from Congo. In 2005, Kabungulu from Hérieters de la Justice, the man who convinced me to become an activist, was murdered, probably because of his activist work. After that I got the news that 56 people in Bunyakiri were killed by a Hutu militia fighting the Congolese government. Among the dead were my sister's husband, Josephine's nephew, the father of Akili (the nephew I brought to Australia) and many other neighbours. What wrong did these poor men, women and children do? I was very choked at their deaths, but I have had to focus on solving my own problems and there was no way I could solve other people's problems.

24

Swept away like a bit of wood

When I bought the house in Sydney it meant I had solved the biggest problem in my life. It was a relief for me. I felt I could have a rest from the pressure of landlords. There has been some damage to our house but no-one tells me to fix it, whereas if I was renting I would be thrown out. My kids, when they were all at home, made a lot of damage. Kids are very careless and they don't care if it is a rental house or not. If they come home late and find the door locked, they are afraid to wake up their parents, so they climb through a window and destroy it to get in.

One night two men broke a window and also got into the house. Luko'o was home alone, in his room, and didn't hear anything because he was listening to music with headphones. When they went upstairs, Luko'o finally heard them and opened his door – to see the two robbers standing there. They got a fright and ran to their car, telling him that if he followed them they would kill him. Luko'o called the police, but when the police arrived and he answered the door they pointed their guns and told *him* to put his hands up! Luko'o said, 'I'm the one who called you!' They were polite to him after that.

Our priority up until now has been paying our mortgage and not spending money on other things. I struggle a lot, but we prefer to drink water and then go to sleep if we can't afford dinner, because paying the mortgage comes first. We decided many times to sell our house and move to a smaller place and pay rent, but we calculated it was not worth it because the mortgage on our house is still less than rents in Sydney.

Josephine and I use virtually all the unemployment benefits from the government to pay the mortgage and we rely on our children for help, although we only get this from our daughters. They give us money straightaway if we are really desperate, Jamaa buys us a 25-kilogram sack of rice, Zawadi buys us a 20-litre container of cooking oil, and Deborah buys us a box of fish, and we grow food in our garden. This is how we survive.

A couple of years after I had been working for the non-profit organisation and just before we bought the house, the organisation lost the contract to settle refugees and the government gave the tender to a private company. All the settlement case workers like me applied for jobs with the new company but only some were successful. Luckily I was kept on as a casual case worker, but I was upset because what I really wanted was a permanent job and to be a case manager.

Then a bad incident occurred. I was assigned to pick up a refugee family arriving at the airport. The family had a sick two-year-old child who had been in hospital in Nairobi before the family came to Australia. After doing a short arrival interview and buying them some food, I went to take them to their short-term accommodation. The father had friends in Sydney and asked if I knew them, and I had been his friends' caseworker when they arrived. We arranged to meet them, then I went home. The next morning I heard the little boy had died.

I was shocked. I had been with them at the airport the night before. I didn't understand how this death could have happened. There was an investigation, but I was never worried I would lose my job because I was sure I had done all the things I had been told to do. The company kept me on as a case worker, but from that time on, I felt the managers were somehow unhappy with me although no-one said what was wrong. When I asked what the problem was, they told me there was no problem.

One problem in my mind was that I was still a casual when I wanted a permanent job, and I started to complain. I complained about my salary, that I was not permanent, that I was receiving no training, and that I did not get a promotion. In May 2008, after two years of complaining, I finally got a full-time permanent job, this time doing community relations work for the company. I was paid $900 per fortnight after tax. It wasn't much money. I was trying to pay a mortgage and had nine children at home, and Josephine wasn't working. One colleague told me, 'Only you are paid this salary. No-one else is paid this little.' So I went to ask for a higher salary.

People did not like me complaining or asking for a higher salary, and they started to say things. Some colleagues started to say negative things about Pygmies. One said, 'Pygmies live in the forest. They are the lowest life in the Congo. They don't go to school and aren't educated.' When I heard this, I confronted the person – a Congolese – who'd said it. 'Why are you talking about Pygmies like this? They are my people,' I told him. He replied, 'I wasn't talking about your people. You are educated – you are not a Pygmy. I was talking about Pygmies elsewhere in Congo.' Then a manager whom I liked a lot called me into his office. 'There's a rumour in the office that you've got a Pygmy smell,' he said. 'Those people are denigrating you, but I know you are a clean person. Keep calm and don't make an issue about this in the office.' Then someone made a comment that I felt was even worse.

The company had sent some employees to get a Diploma in Community Service from a local TAFE college, because they said this would be necessary for their new case manager positions. They didn't send me – I was a case worker, not a case manager. But as I had wanted to become a case manager, I enrolled part-time at another TAFE campus to study for the same diploma, although I had to pay for this myself. I always knew that in Australia I had to improve my education to get ahead, and I really endeavoured to get a university degree. In 2004, not long after I arrived in Sydney, I had started a UniTrack course at the University of Western Sydney, which prepares people who are not quite ready to attend university. Then, in 2006, I got a Certificate in Interpreting and Translating from a TAFE college to help me get work dealing with the African community. I had thought getting my Diploma in Community Services, which I received in May 2009, would help me as well.

After getting my diploma I took it to work and told my manager. I asked him to show it to our senior manager because I thought I should be entitled to a pay rise, now that I had the same qualification as others. My manager showed it to our boss, who said, 'If this is really a diploma, go and find a job somewhere else with it.' I took this comment very personally. I couldn't believe that I had come to Australia and someone had made this comment. It woke me up and I realised that I had forgotten I was still subhuman despite my apparent integration into society. My thoughts flew directly to the early 1970s when my teacher Mr Enoch had beaten me half-dead and nobody had worried. All discriminatory songs of the 1970s returned to my mind: how if a Pygmy wears the same clothes as a Bantu, or goes to school and gets the same diploma, he shouldn't mislead himself that he is a Bantu. I believed that as a Pygmy I could not escape from our curse.

I had already started studying for a Bachelor of Applied Social Science at the local Jansen Newman Institute, but because of the humiliation I decided to stop. I felt convinced that what the Bantus say about Pygmies must be the pure reality, and I didn't have the courage to continue to study anything any more. I felt like going back to Congo, to my previous life. I started to feel social exclusion, even though I was still working, and that there was partiality in the workplace. When I told colleagues I had the right to be treated equally, a workmate from Ethiopia said, 'Did you have that in Africa? In your country?' She thought I was being ungrateful.

The way I had been humiliated went through the Congolese community and they made a lot of comments. When I tried to defend myself to them, I failed. I started to stay away from them and from all those organisations that deal with refugees. It made me think of Mark Twain's quote: 'Keep away from people who try to belittle your ambitions. Small people always do that, but the really great make you feel that you, too, can become great.' It also made me think about how if all the Pygmies died, the Bantu would be left in their world without us. That would solve a lot of problems for everyone. I became so depressed I got high blood pressure and my doctor put me on antidepressants, and I thought about suicide. I felt unable to function in the environment at work, and so in October 2010 my employment was terminated. I was not willing, or able, to continue to perform my duties.

But I was angry and upset, and I lodged a complaint with the government Anti-Discrimination Board about the things that had been said and the way I had been treated. I told a former colleague, an Iranian woman who used to be a case worker, what happened to me. 'Try never to have a problem with your employer in Australia,' she said, 'because they will tell everyone, and you will still have a problem and you'll never get another job.'

The Anti-Discrimination Board did not make a finding in my favour, but I appealed their decision and in April 2011 a mediated settlement between me and the company was arranged. A former colleague advised me, 'Isaac, even I can tell you that you can't win. When you are against a big company like this, don't think you will win. You will stress yourself for nothing.' I could not afford legal advice so I went to Legal Aid and met with a free lawyer. He said, 'You are fighting with someone, but he's got a missile and you've got a Kalashnikov. Do you think you can beat him?' He refused to come to the mediation. He thought I had no chance.

It made me think about what they told me at the workshops I went to in Africa as a representative of APDMAC. They told us, 'Don't be intimidated. Don't be shy. You have to speak loudly about your rights until they listen to you.' And Kabungulu had told me, 'You have to be prepared for a lot of pressure to keep you down.' I wanted to go through with the appeal but I decided that whatever happened I would never complain again.

On the day of the mediation I took the train into the city and went up into a skyscraper. I sat on the end of a big table. I was alone in this room and I felt it. At the opposite end was the mediator. She looked Fijian or Indian. I cannot say that she was on my side or the other side. Her voice was impartial and she didn't take sides. In between us along one side of the table were the people from the company: the general manager, supported by two lawyers – and not lawyers like I had seen at Legal Aid, but lawyers from one of the most powerful law firms in Sydney – and another lady who was taking notes. They were polite and quiet, not aggressive, but I could see that the general manager wanted to get rid of me by any means and that the lawyers were ready for defence.

The mediator was very talented and knew how to reach the hearts of people in conflict. She asked what I wanted and what they wanted, and she helped us reach a settlement. The company paid me some money but I am not allowed to tell anyone how much.

Since I left that job in 2010 I have been unable to find another job. I felt like I was blocked from participating in society. What was my solution? Go back to Congo? I came to Australia for myself, for my safety. *My* life was in danger, not my kids', so I didn't come here to improve the lives of my kids. I was the one who needed integration into Australia. I needed a job! If there was one thing I was sure of, it was that if I was not working that meant I was not useful to anybody and by definition I must be useless and worthless.

All the methods I had used to try to integrate into society failed. All the doors I knocked on were closed to me. I felt exhausted. I appreciated infinitely the Australian government for its hospitality towards my family, and for granting me Australian citizenship for free after it took me from Nairobi at its own expense. It now also gives me unemployment benefits, the dole, but I don't want it. I want to work! When you are included in the labour force you leave home in the morning, have interaction with people, know the things you have to do, and you get your pay. But if you try to get into Australian society without work, then you get swept away like a bit of wood before a wave.

25

In my blood

Josephine and I also started to have a lot of problems at home with the kids. My three eldest daughters always helped us and were never really a problem. The problems started with my middle kids when they became teenagers. We have gone through a lot with them and they have caused too much headache. Really, it is very stressful to look after teenagers because they want freedom, but teenage is a crazy age.

When Wetekay was a teenager and lived at home he wanted to go out at night but did not have a car. I usually go to bed around 10 pm, and by midnight I am deeply asleep. I discovered that Wetekay would wait until I was asleep then take my car and drive into the city or to nightclubs in Kings Cross. And Luko'o nearly drowned when he was about sixteen. We had gone to a beach near Taree, north of Sydney. Luko'o was full of confidence and told us, 'I'm a great swimmer!' He got swept out to sea and was rescued by beach lifeguards. They brought him back out of the ocean with red eyes and breathing heavily.

Our biggest problem was with Bikulo. She is the black sheep of the family and even when she was a girl she had a big personality and was aggressive. When she was sixteen she started going out with friends late at night to clubs and bars, and coming home drunk. She also smoked, even though we forbade smoking in the home because it is bad for the health. One night her friends dumped her on our doorstep. Bikulo was totally drunk, unable to walk or stand, and woke up the whole house to be let inside. I was very angry with her and called the police because I wanted them to witness that she was drunk and to know that someone had obviously bought her alcohol when she was under-age. When the police arrived they said they could not do anything in such cases other than call an ambulance, which is what they did. Bikulo spent that night in hospital.

She came home drunk another time, when Josephine was in New Zealand. I was asleep, and one of her brothers answered the door and started shouting at her, asking what she was doing coming home so late and so drunk and waking everyone up. They started fighting, hitting each other. We all woke up from the noise and went into Bikulo's bedroom, and one of her sisters and another brother also started beating her. I didn't stop my other children from hitting her. Bikulo had three bottles of beer in her bag and I asked her where she got them from and shouted at her. I was angry that she was drunk and so disobedient. The next day someone at school saw Bikulo's wounds and called the police and child welfare, and she was taken to hospital.

The police investigated and said Bikulo should take out an Apprehended Violence Order, an AVO, against me and the sister and two brothers who beat her, and she did. This meant that I was not allowed to mistreat or physically touch her, and that if I did I could be punished by the courts. I have never understood how this could happen. No-one interviewed me or her brothers and sister about what really happened. They just asked Bikulo. We lived together in the same house for two years while she had an AVO against me, her father.

One day while Bikulo had the AVO out against me, she

disappeared. We were worried and reported to the police that she was missing. We eventually managed to speak to her on her mobile phone and we found out that she was in Adelaide. One thousand kilometres away! She told us she had decided to go there for a few days. The police said that when she came back we should tell her to come in to the station and talk to them. When Bikulo returned and we told her, she said, 'I'm not afraid of the police!' The policeman asked where she had been and she replied, 'It's not your business!' He told her everyone had been worried about where she had been staying, but she replied, 'You don't have to know who I was staying with.' After the interview the policeman took me aside and said, 'Be careful with your daughter. This one can create a problem for you.'

When Bikulo came home drunk I would have liked to punish her by leaving her outside in the cold and not letting her in, but the government wouldn't have liked that! The government says it cares about children's welfare, but if it really wanted to look after Bikulo's welfare it would have investigated who gave her the alcohol, who sold her cigarettes and who was taking her out late at night to nightclubs. I was worried about her welfare and wanted the police to investigate these things, but they didn't. She could have been raped!

My other kids have learnt from this. Recently thirteen-year-old Boaz put on his school uniform and left the house to go to school. Later that morning the school rang to say he wasn't in class and asked where he was. Boaz had pretended to go to school, but after going out the front door had crept around the side of the house, in the back door and gone up to his room. Bikulo had bought Jonathan, my grandson, an iPad, but Boaz had taken it and locked himself in his room so he could play with it all day, while we were downstairs. He was being very quiet because he was scared we would catch him. After we got the phone call I went up to his room and found the door locked, and that's when I knew someone was inside. I took the iPad off Boaz and told him he could only use it on weekends. He said, 'It was Bikulo who gave me the iPad, not you! You've got no right to take it. I'll call the police and child welfare and I'll say that you were beating me.' Boaz also told me, 'You didn't learn any lessons from what Bikulo did to you. I want to teach you a second lesson!' He just didn't want to go to school.

Another time at school, Boaz and some Vietnamese boys were talking about pornography using swear words. A teacher told them off and they replied that they would sue the school principal. Someone from the school telephoned me about his behaviour. I told them it was the government's fault because it protects children when they disobey their parents, like it protected Bikulo after she drank alcohol and went out without our permission. If I gave Boaz five smacks he would stop saying these kinds of things at school, but I'm not allowed to do it. In Congo, parents have all the power and kids are more polite and they respect their parents more. If you physically harm your child then according to the law you can be punished, but a little discipline – including smacking or hitting with a stick – can be used by parents. You can't do this to someone else's child, just your own. But it doesn't mean you hate your child!

I accept that I should have intervened when Bikulo was beaten by her siblings, but I feel that the government did not look at all the good things I have done for Bikulo's welfare and the welfare of my other children, like paying for them to attend private schools in Nairobi. What I did not like is that Bikulo is related to me by blood, because she is my daughter, but she is related to the police and child welfare by the law. Blood should be stronger than the law, and if we lose Bikulo – if she dies, or becomes a drunkard – we will be the loser, we will miss her, not the police or child welfare. The police can use their power to punish us but they have no empathy for Bikulo if something happens to her. When parents get cranky with their kids the government punishes, but it doesn't know how much you've done for those kids.

In Congo, poverty keeps people together. Families stay together to eat, to get food, and if you come from a big family you are more likely to eat. There is also no encouragement by the government for children to disobey their parents, by protecting them when they smoke and drink alcohol or go out at night. In Australia, children get their own money from the government, which means they can move out of home. My son Abishay was studying at university and living at home, but moved out because he could get more money from the government.

When Australians ask how many we are in our family and we say 'ten children' everyone is amazed, but my kids think it is not good to have ten children because of this reaction. They want to imitate the society they are living in now, and want only one or two children. Zawadi is now 28 and has already been married for two years but she has no children. She doesn't want any soon, although she said she might have some when she is finished university. She says, 'Look at you, Dad. You had ten children and they caused you so many problems.' Zawadi's husband, a Lebanese Australian, feels the same way. He says he doesn't mind if he never has kids. Jamaa, she is now 30 and is married to a Nigerian and has two children, but she doesn't want any more either. She wants to work. As for Wetekay, who is now 25, well, he just wants to drink and dance. He spends all his money in Kings Cross, nightclubbing.

In my experience, boys do not help their parents much, although all Africans – including Pygmies – want boys. Our sons spend their money on themselves or on their girlfriends. In the Pygmy mentality, we value boys because we think they will bring something to the family, but girls will marry into someone else's family and contribute to that family. If Wetekay comes home when I am not there – because I no longer allow him in the house – everyone is on alert that he might take something. Not just money, but anything that he can sell. One of my daughters said to Mama, 'You were so happy when Wetekay was born because it would extend the family line, but he is stealing from our own house.' Boys forget about their parents. This is why I think valuing boys over girls is not right. I told Josephine that we should go to a lawyer and write a will in case something happens to us. I don't understand why boys should inherit the house – which is what would happen in Congo – and those who are helping us get nothing. I'll make sure that our daughters get the share they deserve if we die.

Even Bikulo has changed positively since she was about nineteen. After the AVO expired in 2013, I went to court to have the whole thing revoked. I wanted my name to be taken out of the government's database so nobody could hold it against me. Bikulo wrote a letter to the court saying that she considered the matter to be finished, and that although she had moved out of home she continued to visit us. The judge was impressed with the letter, and heard my own arguments, and she revoked the order. My family and I, including Bikulo, were very happy. It was a victory on our side. I had felt like the AVO had made me a criminal, and it made me feel powerless towards my children and took away the authority I had in my family, but we had found a judge who listened and heard our cries and worries. After the judge's decision, Bikulo and Zawadi paid for Josephine and me to go on an evening cruise on Sydney Harbour. There were so many enjoyable things, starting with the food, then the music, dancing and beer. We wished we could have stayed on that boat for the whole night.

Like me, Mama is also disappointed in her sons. A few years ago my brother Buhavu sold the land where the Mafuo chiefs are buried, the *buhombe* hill for which my family is the traditional custodian. Buhavu is the one who killed his dog with a panga. There were even some teeth of an old *mwami* still there. Mama was very upset about him selling this land. Buhavu did not have personal custody of that land and had no right to sell it. Mama wanted me to go to court in Congo so the land could be returned to her family. I told her that as she believes in the dead she should ask the dead to talk to Buhavu. The dead chiefs' skulls are supposed to talk, so they could tell Buhavu, 'Don't sell our place.' After hearing that the *buhombe* hill had been sold, Mama's dream is to go back to Congo, return the money to the Bantu people who bought that sacred land, and get it back. It is only the cost of the airfare that is stopping her from returning.

I told Mama this isn't my dream. My dream is to buy a small piece of land, one or two hectares in the countryside where it is calm. Somewhere it is not too hot and not too cold, like in Bunyakiri. Around Lismore or Tweed Heads in northern New South Wales is like this. I would make a small farm with chickens and goats and a garden, and plant African vegetables like cassava, banana trees and pumpkin vines – pumpkin like in Congo, which is much better than what I find here. Then I would forget about Africa and I would live my remaining twenty or thirty years there until I die.

The problem is that Josephine doesn't like the countryside! She doesn't want to be far from her children, especially all of her daughters who live in Sydney. They are all very close and when she gets together with them they talk, talk, talk. Josephine is already living her dream. She likes family a lot and wants to look after her grandchildren, and for her Sydney is the best place in Australia. She won't leave here to go elsewhere. She says, 'If you have something to eat that day, you should be happy,' so for her having the family around and food on the table is enough.

This has never been enough for me. Having a position – a job – and having an active life with others is also important. When you live in the community outside the forest you try to make yourself equal to others and that makes life stressful. In the forest no-one looks down on you. No-one asks you about what you have, because in the forest no-one has anything. The Pygmies who follow this traditional life do not worry about many things, just what they will eat that day. But I do not envy the people who stay in the forest. I can't, because things change in life and we are becoming modernised. No-one who comes out of the forest goes back. There is no point envying people who stay where they are. The people who stay do so because it is simply their habit and they do not want to change their lifestyle.

But I think about being a Pygmy a lot, at least ten times a day. For me being a Pygmy is natural. I can't lose my nature just because I am out of the forest, or because of living a new life. I was born like this, it's in my blood and I can't change it. My hope is that by reading this memoir people understand that Pygmies and indigenous people everywhere have the abilities of other people. What we do not have are opportunities. We have been disadvantaged by the human system, let me even say oppressed. That is why I wanted to tell my story, to educate people about Pygmies.

This is my memoir as a Pygmy and, if you read this book, you will learn that all the Pygmies are not in the forest, not naked, and not beggars. You will understand that there has been a big change in the Pygmy lifestyle. We are all human and you are just like me. What we have in common is the capacity for thinking. There are things I can do that you can't do, but we all have the ability to learn. What we have in common is the aspiration to discover new things in life.

Epilogue

Michael Nest

At the time of publication Isaac had not found another job, and this continues to affect his morale. In typical Congolese, entrepreneurial fashion, however, Isaac is exploring other options. He obtained a licence to be a coordinator for family daycare, a popular business for migrant women who get government subsidies to look after other people's children in their own homes. Coordinators organise paperwork, insurance and payments on behalf of the women, and Isaac remains hopeful that he may be able to obtain two or three clients. He also obtained a bus driver's licence, and applied for a position as a caseworker at Sydney's Villawood Immigration Detention Centre. Isaac still owns a small truck that operates out of Bukavu, and he mulls over how he could obtain investment capital to import trucks from China to expand this business and generate income. His latest idea came from the Ugandan Ambassador to Russia, whom Isaac sat next to on an Emirates flight. The ambassador suggested that Isaac start a business advising and supporting students from Uganda and elsewhere in Africa to attend university in Australia, and Isaac is busy thinking how he could bring this idea to fruition.

Isaac's all-consuming battle to get a job or start a business was upended in January 2014. He and Josephine had many hopes for their sixth child and third son, Abishay, who was studying at Macquarie University. He had obtained his private pilot's licence, and had given presentations about Pygmies at school and at a City of Fairfield event. At university Abishay started to develop a mental illness, which included fixating on discrimination against Pygmies, and he started drinking. He dropped out of university and moved home, where Isaac told him to stop drinking. This created conflict and Abishay moved out. One night the police telephoned: Abishay had been found in the street and they took him to a psychiatric hospital in North Sydney. Josephine and Isaac brought him home but Abishay locked himself away in his room, not coming out for days at a time. When he did come out, he kept asking his father, 'Why are we [Pygmies] so discriminated against?' Finally, Abishay decided he wanted to go back to Africa, to the Kasachi Forest, the ancestral forest, and experience life there – surely with a view to exploring his roots and making peace with his heritage. His sister Bikulo, to whom he was very close, gave him the money for an airfare. Back in Bukavu, Abishay met up with family friends and went swimming in Lake Kivu, where he drowned. Lake Kivu is notorious for methane gas bubbling up from the lake bottom: swimmers can enter a cloud of gas sitting on the surface of the water, not realising they have entered a zone with no oxygen and this, apparently, is what happened to Abishay.

His death has had a wrenching impact. Isaac is devastated, and he tells me that Abishay now appears frequently in Josephine's dreams, often in the kitchen at their Canley Vale home protesting that he does not want to do the dishes. Bikulo, the sister who gave Abishay the money for his airfare, went to bed comatose for several days after her brother's death.

Despite this tragedy and other struggles, telling and recording this oral history has had a positive impact on Isaac. When we first started meeting in the café in September 2012, Isaac barely said the word 'Pygmy' and when he did, he said it in a low voice. I copied his behaviour, assuming he did not want people to know that we were talking about Pygmies. I began to think this was silly – we were trying to write a memoir of a Pygmy after all – but decided it was his prerogative to talk like this. A good five months into the project I noticed a change. Isaac started to say 'Pygmy' more frequently and in the same tone of voice as the rest of our conversation. He no longer cared who overheard us or what they thought.

While still looking for a publisher we started to do some publicity about the project. Our first engagement was giving a couple of talks for Refugee Week at public libraries on the New South Wales north coast. The audiences were friendly and eager to learn about refugees, and there was an air of wonder that a Pygmy had come to town. Several people asked to have their photo taken with Isaac and there were many questions, mostly about life in the jungle and from people curious that Isaac seemed so reconciled to a non-traditional life outside the forest.

In the car on the way back to Sydney from the north coast Isaac was silent. I wondered what he was thinking and asked how he thought the presentations went. After the longest pause he said, 'This getting out and meeting people, talking to them, this is the feeling of integration.'

Glossary

Alliance des Forces Démocratiques pour la Libération du Congo. The French term for the Alliance of Democratic Forces for the Liberation of the Congo. The Alliance was the collection of foreign and Congolese forces that started a military campaign against the government of President Mobutu in 1996 and eventually took control of Congo in 1997.

APDMAC. Action d'Appui Pour la Promotion des Droits de Minorités Autochtones en Afrique Centrale, or Action to Support the Promotion of Indigenous Minority Rights in Central Africa. APDMAC is the non-profit organisation established by Pygmies in Eastern Congo, including Isaac, to improve the status and treatment of Pygmies. APDMAC continues to function today.

Bantu. The word used to describe the majority of black people from East, Central and Southern Africa. There is also a linguistic category of languages called 'Bantu languages' found in this region. In these languages the word Bantu itself means 'human'. Pygmies speak Bantu languages, but they are not considered to be Bantu. The term Bantu has come to have connotations of race.

BaTembo. A numerically small tribe, with many Pygmy members, found in the provinces of North Kivu and South Kivu in Eastern Congo. The tribe traces its ancestry to Katembo – a Bantu man from the Hunde tribe who married a Pygmy woman about 400 years ago. Isaac is a member of this tribe, as well as being a Pygmy, so he is a BaTembo Pygmy.

Buhombe. The term used in Isaac's part of Congo to refer to the grave site of a Bantu chief. *See also* Muhombe.

Héritiers de la Justice. A Congolese non-profit organisation working in the area of human rights.

Hunde. A numerically large tribe found in Eastern Congo. The language of this tribe is also called Hunde.

Hutu: A socio-economic category used in Rwanda, Burundi and DR Congo. Historically, Hutu and the related category of Tutsi were mostly used to refer to a person's status in terms of wealth, and children inherited their status from their fathers. Generally, Hutu refers to a person who farms and possesses few cattle, and Tutsi refers to a person who possesses wealth in terms of cattle, but there are exceptions to this. A Hutu's status could change if his wealth changes, e.g., if he becomes rich, or married well, he might be considered a Tutsi. Usage also varies by region. Congolese also sometimes use 'Hutu' to refer to former Rwandan government soldiers and génocidaires who fled to Congo after the genocide in Rwanda in 1994, even though not all Hutus participated in the genocide. Hutu is not a tribal identity.

Interahamwe. The name given to Hutu extremists who carried out many of the killings during the 1994 genocide in Rwanda. Thousands of members of Interahamwe groups fled to Congo after the genocide when Tutsi rebels took control of Rwanda. In Congo the Interahamwe regrouped inside refugee camps, controlling refugees and the distribution of aid, and launching attacks on Tutsis.

Kirundi. The national language of Burundi.

KiTembo. The language spoken by the BaTembo tribe. KiTembo is a dialect of the Hunde language. It is Isaac's first language.

Mafuo Chiefdom. The traditional country of Isaac's mother's family. The Mafuo Chiefdom is the chiefdom that surrounds Bunyakiri.

Mai Mai. The name given to various small, armed militias operating in Eastern Congo.

Mobutu. President Mobutu was the president of Congo from 1965 to 1997.

Muhombe. The name for the custodian of the graves of Bantu chiefs.

Isaac's father's family traditionally had this role in their traditional country. *See also* Buhombe.

Muzungu. The word for 'white man' or 'white person' in Swahili.

Mwami. A word used in several African languages for a village chief or a king.

Pygmy. The generic name given to populations of short stature (typically less than 150 centimetres for adult men and less than 145 centimetres for adult women) living across Central Africa. Pygmies do not have one of the medical conditions that cause dwarfism – their short stature is a normal genetic variation. Pygmies have social and cultural attributes that distinguish them from non-Pygmy populations. The term Pygmy has come to have connotations of race. In some countries the term 'Pygmy' is considered pejorative.

RCD. Rassemblement Congolaise pour la Démocratie, or Congolese Union for Democracy. One of the major rebel armed groups opposing the Congolese government between 1998 and 2003.

Shi. A large tribe found in Eastern Congo. The language of this tribe is also called Shi.

Swahili. A common language in East Africa and Eastern Congo.

Tutsi: A socio-economic category used in Rwanda, Burundi and D.R. Congo. Historically, and like the related category of Hutu, Tutsi was mostly used to refer to a person's status in terms of wealth and children inherited their status from their fathers. Generally, Tutsi refers to a person who possesses wealth in terms of cattle, but there are exceptions to this. A Tutsi's status may change if his wealth changes, e.g., if a he becomes poor he might be considered a Hutu. Usage also varies by region. Congolese sometimes use 'Tutsi' to refer to any Congolese with Rwandan ancestry, regardless of whether that person's ancestors were considered Tutsi in Rwanda. Tutsi is not a tribal identity.

List of recurring people

Bikulo. One of Isaac's daughters, his seventh child. Bikulo took out an Apprehended Violence Order against Isaac and two of her siblings.

Boaz. One of Isaac's sons, his ninth child.

Buhavu. Isaac's younger, and only surviving, brother. It was Buhavu who killed his dog with a panga and who sold the buhombe land.

Jamaa. One of Isaac's daughters, his first child.

Josephine. Isaac's wife. Isaac's first girlfriend was also called Josephine.

Kabungulu. The activist working for the Congolese non-profit organisation Héritiers de la Justice, who convinced Isaac to work for Pygmy rights.

Kangene. A Pygmy elder from the Bunyakiri area, related to Isaac through clan ties. Kangene was one of the first Pygmies to receive some education (in the 1950s). He was also one of the first to campaign for Pygmy rights.

Lucien. A Rwandan man who was a friend and business partner of Isaac's from the pharmaceutical sector. Isaac sheltered Lucien when he escaped violence in Rwanda in 1994.

Moni. A Congolese Tutsi man who was a friend and neighbour of Isaac's in the 1980s, and then worked for Isaac as a pharmaceuticals selling agent.

Monsieur François. A Belgian man who managed the tea and cinchona plantation in South Kivu Province where Isaac's father worked in the 1970s.

Mr Katipula. A former teacher of Isaac's who lived in Bunyakiri. Mr Katipula helped Isaac several times, especially by giving him a big white hen.

Professor Job. A former teacher and mentor of Isaac, with whom Isaac stayed when he attended high school in Bukavu.

Sinafasi. A Pygmy activist from the Ituri region in Eastern Congo. Sinafasi was an executive committee member of APDMAC.

Tschambu. A former nurse whom Isaac hired to manage his Bunyakiri pharmacy. Tschambu was tortured by RCD rebel forces.

Tuteene. Josephine's brother and a current executive member of APDMAC.

Wetekey. One of Isaac's sons, his fourth child.

Zania. One of Isaac's sisters. Zania died giving birth to twins.

Zawadi. One of Isaac's daughters, his third child.

Endnotes

Introduction

Page 2: **'The zoo director's intention was to provoke New Yorkers into reflecting on Darwin's …'** For the story of Ota Benga see *Ota Benga: The Pygmy in the zoo* by Phillips Verner Bradford and Harvey Blume, St Martins Press, New York, 1992.

Page 2: **'A century later the international media reported that armed militias waging war …'** For an article about this story, see 'Congo rebels are eating Pygmies, UN says' by James Astill, *The Guardian*, 9 January 2003.

Page 9: **'There are no Pygmy authors and no authors … not for their own sake.'** This quote is from Jan Vansina's *Paths in the Rainforests: Toward a history of political tradition in equatorial Africa*, University of Wisconsin Press, Madison, 1990, p. 29.

Chapter 2

Page 19: **'Bantus from many tribes came into our land centuries ago, but before the seventeenth century …'** BaTembo Pygmies are one of eighteen different Pygmy populations across Central Africa. Scholars think that the ancestral Pygmy population diverged from non-Pygmies about 70,000 years ago. It is not clear where this ancient population emerged or when either population migrated into the Congo Basin, but there is archaeological evidence that humans have lived in the forests of Central Africa for at least 40,000 years. Between 3000 and 5000 years ago non-Pygmy populations took up agriculture, whereas Pygmies retained their hunter-gatherer way of life – although depending on the availability of food, most Pygmies migrate seasonally out of the forest to tend crops on the farms of non-Pygmy communities. Isaac is impatient with scholarly uncertainty about Pygmy history: local mythology in his part of Congo places Pygmies firmly in the forest, first.

Page 19: **'Katembo and his wife made a new settlement at Mbo'o Hill, in an area now called Ufamandu …'** The history of the BaTembo was researched by the Congolese scholar Mapendano Pindo, who published his research in *Essai d'Histoire politique des BaTembo*, Institut Supérior Pédagogique de Bukavu, South Kivu, 1977 (p. 31).

Page 20: **'Thousands of years ago Pygmies had their own language, but today Pygmies speak …'** Linguistically, BaTembo Pygmies are part of the Pygmy group defined by the language family 'Bantu JD50: Shi-Hunde'.

Chapter 17

Page 141: **'They were all trying to get to Kisangani, to a refugee camp called Tingi-Tingi …'** No-one knows for sure how many civilians were killed in massacres around this time, like the one at Tchambutsha or the even bigger massacre that occurred at Tingi-Tingi, which was the destination of many of those killed at Tchambutsha. While some people trekking through the forest died from starvation, disease and exhaustion, it is clear from the accounts of refugees, humanitarian organisations, diplomats and former soldiers that tens of thousands of refugees were murdered by the Alliance. The total number killed by the Alliance is possibly around 150,000. For a compelling account by a Rwandan refugee who walked through the forest to escape the Alliance, see *Surviving the Slaughter: The ordeal of a Rwandan Refugee in Zaire*, by Béatrice Umutesi, University of Wisconsin Press, Madison, Wisconsin, 2004.

Chapter 25

Page 218: **'If I gave Boaz five smacks he would stop saying these kinds of things at school …'** African immigrants' use of corporal punishment on their children, which is common in Africa, is a perennial issue in child welfare circles and African communities in Australia. When parents hit their children and the Australian government intervenes, the African parents think the government is taking sides against them and is deliberately trying to undermine their authority. They cannot comprehend that the government can interfere in their families or take away their children. African parents are also dubious about the 'child welfare' argument. As they see it, they hit their kids to discourage them from doing things that are harmful to their welfare, such as drinking, smoking, having a boyfriend or skipping school. Following government intervention, or an Apprehended Violence Order, the parents sometimes stop disciplining their children altogether because the only tool they know – corporal punishment – is against the law. Their kids' response is to run amok. They can tell their parents are scared of the government and they think the government is on the side of children.

Other great memoirs from Finch Publishing

Marzipan & Magnolias
Elizabeth Lancaster
ISBN: 9781921462207

When the Bough Breaks
Joanne W Jones
ISBN: 9781921462221

False Start
Mark O'Flynn
ISBN:9781921462894

Catch Up With the Sun
Heidi Douglas

ISBN:9781921462368

The Bouncer
Heath Lander
ISBN:9780987419651

Green Vanilla Tea
Marie Williams

ISBN: 9781921462993

Spinifex Baby

Karen Haarland

ISBN: 9781925048155

Boyfriends We've All Had
Mandy Nolan
ISBN: 9781921462825

What I Would Do if I Were You

Mandy Nolan

ISBN: 9781925048131

9/11 and the Art of Happiness
Simon Kennedy
ISBN: 9781925048087